Baby's Growth

Age	Weight		Height	
	lbs.	ozs.	ft.	ins.
one week	8	14		21
two weeks	9	5		21½
one month	10	9		23
two months	13	0		24
three months				25
four months	16	2		26
five months				
six months				
seven months	20	12		
eight months				
nine months				
ten months				
eleven months				
one year	24			30
2 yrs.	29		34	

Baby Arrives

at Los Cerritos Maternity Hosp.
on April 12, 1947
at 9:00 o'clock A. m.

Doctor Raymond A. Tr

Nurse

Baby's Home

418 E. Arist Street
Long Beach, Calif.
Phone - 684-370

117 W. 4th
Long Beach, Calif.
Phone - 621-563

The sky is filled with stars
Invisible by day.

Henry Wadsworth Longfellow

MY BOOK _____

Indeed I had not much wit, yet I was not an idiot — my wit was according to my years.

Some censuring readers will scornfully say. "Why hath this lady writ her own life? Since no one cares to know whose daughter she was or whose wife she is, or how she was bred, or how she lived, or what humor or disposition she was of?" I answer that it is true, that 'tis to no purpose to the readers, but it is to the Authoress, because I write it for my own sake, not theirs.

Margaret Cavendish 1655

The Fairy Tale Girl

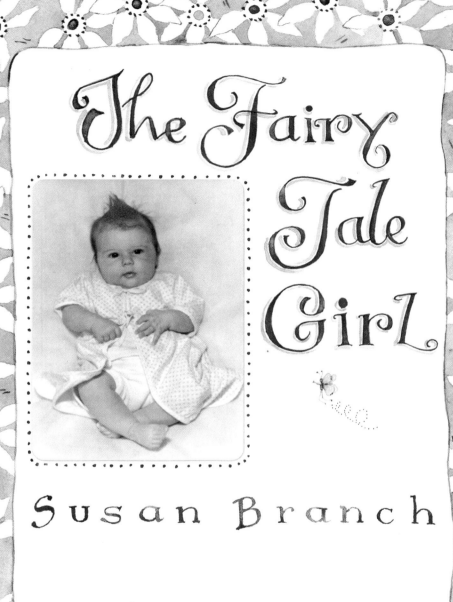

Susan Branch

SPRING STREET *Publishing*

MARTHA'S VINEYARD · MASSACHUSETTS

Spring Street Publishing
P O B O X 2 4 6 3
VINEYARD HAVEN, MA
0 2 5 6 8
sales@springstreetpublishing.com

FIRST   EDITION
ISBN 978-0-9960440-1-1
Library of Congress Control Number
2015908280

10 9 8 7 6 5 4 3 2 1

RRD-IN
PRINTED IN THE
UNITED STATES OF AMERICA

Dedication

This book is dedicated to the wonderful people who made the formative years in my long-ago and far-away "other life" so much fun and provided the fodder that kept my diaries interesting ～ especially Diana Bowlby, Janet Haley, Karen Bennett, Fernando Celis, and the always-creative Tuesday Girls. To Beverly and Jim Smith, John and Carol King, and the ever-patient Elaine Sullivan. And of course, to Cliff. Dearest love to my parents and my siblings ～ I feel so lucky I landed in the same house with them. And in loving remembrance of my grandmother, John Stillman, and Russ and Betty Branch. To my kitties and the person who invented tea, and especially to the darling man in my "real life" who loves me just the way I am (because at this point he's figured out there's really nothing he can do about it). ♥

So come with me where dreams are born & time is never planned.
J.M. Barrie

DISCLAIMER

Truth, in her dress, finds facts too tight.
In fiction, she moves with ease.
♥ Rabindranath Tagore

There is a lovely word, "verisimilitude," (say it three times, and each time you will love it a little bit more) which the dictionary defines as "the appearance of being true or real," recently shortened and clarified most adorably by Stephen Colbert as "truthiness." Though my diaries were my guides while I wrote these books, verisimilitude was my intention. As was suggested by Emily Dickinson when she said, "Tell all the truth but tell it slant," I took the artistic liberty of arranging certain facts to suit my purpose ～ which is to entertain. Some people (mostly me, of course) should be pro-tected ～ the truly innocent should not be dragged through the detritus of an author's recounted (or restructured) memories. I am blessed with the characters in this book in more ways than one, first off, I love them no matter what they've done (mostly because of what they've done) and secondly, most of them are alive and kicking and I want to stay in their good graces. Life has been wonderful so far, I would hate to ruin it now.

Friends～they are kind to each other's hopes
& cherish each other's dreams.
Henry David Thoreau

Preface

...me in great ways – wonder how
a writer writes. What starts them
where do they begin?

9:22 am Jan. 17, 1978 Tuesday

From my diary

Everyone has a bit of a fairy tale in them. I've discovered the full story is much easier to see when looking back rather than while the tale is being written. In fact, the thing I like most about growing older is finally getting a handle on what the heck was going on back then.

And here's what I found out so far: Sometimes, what looks like the bitter end, is just the beginning. Like in a fairy tale, where all things are possible, loss very often turns into a gift. Loneliness is probably the way we get our wings. And heartache and rejection can evolve into inspiration. Someday you might even turn around and be grateful. You might. It's possible. It happened to me.

Based on the diaries I've kept since I was in my 20s, *The Fairy Tale Girl* is an age-old story of love and loss, mystery and magic that begins in a geranium-colored house in California and ends up, surprisingly, like any good fairy tale, on the right side of the rabbit hole ～ in a small cottage in the woods on the island of Martha's Vineyard. How I got there, I will never really understand. But I have no doubt it happened just the way it was supposed to.

The Fairy Tale Girl began as just one volume, but by the time it was finished (I didn't want to leave out any of the good stuff) it had grown to almost the size of my old *Webster's Dictionary*, so I divided it into two books: *The Fairy Tale Girl* is book one, and book two will be *Martha's Vineyard, Isle of Dreams*. And since I like to do things somewhat backward and make them as confusing as possible, both of these books are actually prequels to my last book, *A Fine Romance, Falling in Love with the English Countryside* (published in 2013).

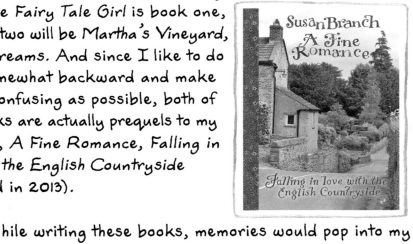

While writing these books, memories would pop into my head at every time of day and night ～ you know you're in the zone when you find yourself naked and drying off but you don't remember getting into the shower . . . there were scraps of paper all over the house with scribbled notes on them. But this is my favorite: I was on my morning walk out through the woods to the sea, and it was SO beautiful, I needed to write down the descriptive words first hand, while I was there, smelling the salt and the sea, feeling the breeze, and hearing the different birds, while watching the ferry dip through the waves on its way to the Cape. I had no phone, but a pen in my pocket, and no paper . . . so I chose a nice white seashell. This is how I tried to tell my story, so you would feel that you were there with me.

So come with me, dear readers, back to the olden days, to the 1900s, where men were men and girls were girls . . . You won't need a seatbelt for this time travel, which is good, because where we're going they haven't been invented yet.

Everyone's life is a fairy tale written by God's fingers.
♥ Hans Christian Andersen

See you later bookie poo — if anyone ever tries to read you, you let out a scream please!
Dec. 27, 1979 —   Thursday — Well,

Dear Diary

THE FAIRY TALE GIRL

December 26, 1957

This is my brand new diary, I got it for Christmas. It is the property of Susan Anne Stewart who is 10½ years old and lives on Claire Avenue in Reseda, California. If you are not me and you are reading this, you are in big trouble. If you broke the lock I will tell Mom. Put it down right now.

Mom says a diary is a place to keep secrets. Here's one, I told Karen, but that's all - a chain is the best lager for hopscotch. Try to use a rock and it will bounce.

FAST FORWARD 25 YEARS!

10

Chapter One
Running Away

*W*hen the dance was over she curtsied, and when the King looked round again she had vanished and none knew whither.
Brothers Grimm

*M*arch 4, 1982 OK— TWA flight 74 is still on the tarmac waiting to taxi. It's about 10:30 pm, we were supposed to leave LA a half hour ago, I wish we could get this thing in the air & get it over with. Diana brought me to the airport — we cried almost the whole way & I'm still crying, half because of him, half because I'm leaving home & half because I'm on this plane by myself. That's too many halves but you understand dear diary. I'm doing the right thing, but I feel terrible.

I was alone and brokenhearted that winter night in 1982 when my red-eye from Los Angeles to Boston finally took off. Even on a good day, I was never a happy flyer. Back in the years when I still did it (I don't anymore, having come to my senses), I would spread the fear around by begging the person next to me to hold my hands during takeoff and landing. Young, old, man, woman, friend or stranger, in my hour of need, it didn't matter. People were amazingly nice about it. I'm pretty sure they wanted to hold hands too but they were probably too polite to ask. I was too scared to be polite. And, I'm happy to tell you, in all those years, no one ever said no. Even with my clammy hands — which had to be the worst part for them — no one ever made a face or wiped their hands on their clothes in front of me.

My most memorable hand-holding victim was a nun, back when they still wore black and white habits. We were sitting next to each other on my very first flight ever—LA to Mexico City. She was fingering her rosary beads but that didn't stop me from asking if I could please hold her hands while the plane took off. "Of course you can, dear." She said, taking my hands in hers. (I really liked them *both* to be held.) She was extra-perfect as wind beneath our wings, plane-protection provider, and prayer center. Few seatmates offered this many benefits.

I always wished I could go up front, knock on the door of the cockpit, and have a chat with the captain. Ask if he had brothers and sisters, was he married, did he have children. Smell his breath a little and look at his pupils. I would have felt so much better.

Walking down the aisle, I assessed my chances of landing in Boston in one piece by looking into the faces of the other passengers to see if anyone stood out as a "loser." I worried about being dragged down in the wake of someone else's destiny. It was always hard to tell, but that night they looked pretty good ～ no drool, greasy hair, or obvious food stains on their clothes. Very few things could take my mind from the misery of running away from home, which is what I was doing, but flying was definitely one of them.

BABY, BABY, CAN'T YOU HEAR MY HEART BEAT...

12

Everything else I could do to endure the torment of flying had been done. I was somewhat of an expert at it by now: I was strapped in my lucky seat ~ last row, right side if you're facing forward (what made it lucky is that I hadn't died in it yet) ~ my shoes were off, my clammy feet were clad in thick cotton socks and wrapped in an airline blanket. I put on my headphones, turned up the Walkman and clutched a pillow for my damp hands. I was ready as I'd ever be.

As we went screaming down the runway ~ nose up, wheels up, belly up, floor at a ridiculous 30-degree angle, Steppenwolf howled in my ear, "Get your motor running, head out on the highway . . ." The music drowned out the apt-to-be-misconstrued-by-me wheel-lifting, gear-grinding, acceleration noise of the engines. If we were going to crash, I wanted to be the last to know.

"... Born to be wi - i - i - i - ild . . ." ♫

Up into the black, starry night we went. I looked out the window to see the wing silhouetted against the glittering lights of Los Angeles. A long line of headlight beams and red taillights snaked up and down Pacific Coast Highway. As the plane rattled higher I reached up and turned off the overhead light and checked the engines for sparks or flames. As the oldest of eight children and parent-appointed "safety monitor," keeping people alive had been part of my childhood responsibilities.

13

I gazed across the miles of city lights. Everyone I loved was down there: my mom and dad; my brothers and sisters; all my best friends; Cliff, the guy I thought I would spend my life with; his parents; my house; my kitty, Pooh. Tears filled my eyes as everything I knew and loved dropped away beneath me.

The plane bumped higher through turbulence. I clutched the armrests (if I was going down I was taking the seat with me). I looked at my watch ~ five long hours to Boston.

Just when you think you have everything figured out, you discover you know nothing at all. ♥

 My best friend, Diana, had driven me to the airport.

"Are you sure you want to do this?" she asked, furrowing her brow. "You don't think it's, like," she hesitated, "overkill?"

"Overkill?" What kind of word was that? "Are you kidding?" Diana had been right there while I was getting my heart broken. She saw the whole thing, she knew I had to do something drastic. She just didn't want me to go.

"It's only for three months," I said, trying to sound like I knew what I was doing. "It's not forever. Don't cry ~ you're making me cry."

I teetered on the verge of saying, "Let's go home," but then I remembered, I had no home.

"I wish you could come with me," I said, but I didn't really. As nervous as I was, and as much as I loved her, I wanted to go alone. I wanted to cut myself away from everything. I was sick of talking about it, sick of hearing about it, sick of this breakup being my only life, day after day for the last six months. Anyway, Diana had a boyfriend, she had a job, she was a baby nurse, she was loved, and people depended on her. She had a life, whereas I, on the other hand, didn't.

She tried to laugh. "I know you're desperate, otherwise you'd never fly cross-country by yourself." The plane began to board, I had to go, we hugged. "Write me! Call!" she shouted as I walked away. Like I wouldn't.

It's funny what you remember when your life comes crashing down around you.

Six months earlier, I was sitting on the rug in the front hall of my house. My kitty, Pooh, was curled up on the stair next to me, dinner was in the oven, Cliff was due home soon. I had just finished sketching a jack-rabbit on the wall in front of me.

I'd never drawn on a wall before, but I had a new hobby of drawing and painting and this idea of a rabbit jumping out of a border of cattails and up the stairs toward the guest room. Maybe it would work, and maybe it wouldn't. If I made a mess of it, I could just paint over it.

I'd already chosen the colors, a reddish brown for his fur and silver for his long whiskers. But before I could paint a single brushstroke, the marriage I thought would last for a lifetime was suddenly over. And the wall, with the bunny, went with it.

Ever since then, I'd been in that empty space between realizing my life would never be the same and figuring out what could be done about it. The worst part was the uncertainty. Nothing made sense, I'd been crying for six months, and I didn't even have my own phone number and address anymore. He had them.

*W*hile I was face down crying into the sofa, my husband Cliff, 29 years old and newly liberated, was frolicking around our small town in his fast car with his new blonde girlfriend, Kimmi (not Kim, Kĭmmĭ, presumably with little hearts over the i's). She had moved into the house Cliff and I built together where I thought we'd live until we had to put in an escalator to get up the long stairs to the front door.

I saw them in town ~ me, the thing that crawled from the sea; them, frisky lovers out for an afternoon of tennis, frozen yogurt, and shopping ~ and that's when I knew I had to go. Our town was too small for the three of us.

I didn't know when I got on the plane that you couldn't run away from a broken heart. I thought you could, but no, sad to say, a broken heart goes where you go. I had a lot to learn and now, finally, at the age of 33, I was taking my first baby steps into the real world ~ like a person pushed off the Titanic being yelled at to SWIM.

17

For the last 10 years, lulled by love, a wedding ring, and a belief in forever after, I had done a stupid thing. I had broken the cardinal rule and put all my eggs in one basket, and as it turns out the basket was his. He had no more use for it and seemingly tossed it out the window of his red Ferrari somewhere on the road between Santa Barbara and Big Sur. I pictured it flying out the window, slamming onto the blacktop, hurtling over the bluff, hitting rocks, flipping and bouncing and pounding all the way down the mountain until the broken jagged pieces of everything that mattered rolled across the sand and into the sea where they floated away forever.

It was no one's fault but my own. I'd married without a contingency plan.

As a child I thought life would be easy: grow up, fall in love, get a little house, plant some roses, live happily ever after. What could be simpler? It always worked that way in the movies.

And, for a while, that's exactly how it was.

CHAPTER TWO

AND SO IT BEGAN

A safe fairyland is unknown in all worlds.
                              J.R.R. Tolkien

I met Cliff in 1971 when Diana and I moved from the San Fernando Valley, a suburb of Los Angeles, to the small college town of San Luis Obispo. A week after we got there, I answered an ad for a record-department clerk in a store downtown called Stereo West.

When I arrived for the interview, I was greeted by a kid who looked to be about 15, sitting behind a record counter, wearing a Black Sabbath T-shirt and headphones, reading MAD magazine. He glanced up, pulled the headphone from one ear so that I could give him my name and tell him why I was there. He dropped the headphone back in place, pointed and said, "Straight back, top of the stairs."

Job interviews made me nervous, I was only 23, but this little kid made me feel old. I hoped I was going to get *his* job. I could see I had all the qualifications needed to handle it.

I walked toward the stairs and noticed that the store sold a lot more than records. There was a glassed-in sound-proof room in the back with customers trying out different speakers. Displays were stacked with stereo equipment, turntables, tuners, and amplifiers. The two salesmen behind the other counter were in their early 20s, wearing bell-bottoms, with lots of hair, handlebar mustaches, and long sideburns. The carpet was orange shag, the walls were rough-hewn barn wood; on one of them hung a clock in the shape of a gold peace symbol. As I climbed the stairs, past framed posters of Cream and Jimi Hendrix, the music played,

♫ ". . .Goin'up to the spirit in the sky . . ." ♪

I really hoped I would get this job.

On the landing, a thin girl with dark hair stepped out of a cubbyhole office with a small wiry dog close behind. She introduced herself as Elaine, the dog as Boxcar and said, "Susan, right?" I nodded, "Yes. Sue." She tapped on the office door next to hers, peeked in, and said, "Hey, Cliff, your ten o'clock is here."

A clean-shaven guy with thick brown hair stood up ~ an all-American boy who looked a lot like Jeff Bridges, wearing rust-colored cords, gray tennis shoes, and a brown Stereo West T-shirt. His left arm was in a hospital-green sling from wrist to shoulder, held together with wide Velcro straps. We introduced ourselves. He was

Cliff Branch. I was Sue Stewart. He motioned for me to sit down, which I did, on a short little sofa with no feet I thought he might have found next to a dumpster somewhere (a common place for us to get our furniture in those days). I sat up straight, pushed my bangs back, rubbed my damp hands down the sides of my dress, and tried to look perky, like Mary Tyler Moore.

I didn't know it at the time, but Cliff, at 21, was already gaining a reputation as a sort of self-made marketing genius. He and his

22-year-old business partner, Tom Spalding, had started Stereo West two years before. It was one of the first mail-order stereo businesses in the United States and was growing by leaps and bounds because baby boomers did not want the kind of big wooden "hi-fi" boxes our parents had. We wanted cool component music systems. Cliff and Tom put Stereo West in the *Whole Earth Catalog*, and it was making them a little bit famous.

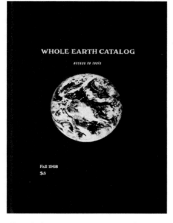

After some small talk, Cliff began to ask me questions and tried to take notes on my application with his bad arm, but the sling he was wearing made it awkward. He looked up, cocked his head at me, glanced at his arm, and said, "Broke my shoulder. Dirt bike accident. Motocross race."

"Oh, that's too bad." I was unable to think of one cute or witty remark to say to him that would for sure not turn him against me. "You shouldn't be on one of those things" wouldn't have been good.

I answered his questions, trying to sound like I knew some-thing about music, which I didn't think I did, even though I could sing every word to every song on the radio. I didn't own a stereo myself, so I tossed off names (I memorized and said over and over to myself because I knew I'd be nervous) like Cat Stevens and Linda Ronstadt.

Suddenly a look of frustration rippled across his face. The sling was slowing him down, he couldn't write. He dropped the pen on the desk, reached up quickly with his right hand, and tore apart the Velcro strips that kept his arm confined.

Rip, riiiiip ~ he pulled the sling off his neck and tossed it aside. He didn't even look at me ~ just picked up the pen and went back to taking notes using his freed bad arm.

That was interesting, I thought, jumping a bit with just the tiniest little heart ping. He's kind of a maniac.

SEE? RIGHT THERE. THAT'S THE KIND of THINKING THAT GETS A GIRL IN TROUBLE.

I answered all his questions. He was pleasant, but a little distracted. He didn't seem like a person who wasted time on small talk. When he was finished, we stood up and he said he'd be in touch, he'd be making his decision later that day or the next.

I looked up at him and said as sweetly as my natural impatience and high hopes would allow, "Well, I hope it's me and I hope it's today."

He laughed ~ his blue eyes twinkled as he reached behind me to open the door: It was the first time I felt like he saw me.

For the rest of the day I hung around the phone, wondering if he'd call. When Diana got home from school I was jumping up and down. I got the job! We could pay the rent! I'd start work the next Monday.

"Lookit that cutie pie down there," I said, rummaging through Diana's long blond hair to find her ear, speaking into it loudly and trying not to cause hearing loss.

We were perched on stools at the far end of a dark, smokey bar crowded with beer bottles, cocktail glasses, ashtrays, and noisy people. Across the dance floor packed with gyrating kids, Leon Russell's "Delta Lady" was being performed on stage by a live band ∼ electric guitars, bass, drums, and a pounding piano. The sound coming from the big black speakers was deafening, and everyone had to yell to be heard.

"Which one?" she hollered back, her eyes darting from person to person along the length of the bar looking for the cutie pie.

"Second seat from the end with the dark hair, the one laughing."

She stood up on the rung of her stool to get a better view.

"Get down!" I whacked her leg with the back of my hand. "He'll see you."

She didn't care. She was up and scanning the bar, sun-kissed tan set off perfectly by her white miniskirt and yellow beaded sweater.

"Oh, yeah, he IS cute." She plopped back down, leaned in to me, and yelled, "Go ask him to dance!"

I looked back down the bar. He was surrounded by people. "Are you crazy?" I hollered. "No way. I'm not going down there."

"Want me to ask him for you?" (She was half off the stool.)

I grabbed her arm. "No!"

"Don't worry. I won't ask him to dance. I'll just go get him and bring him back."

I looked at her for a couple of seconds. There is no one I trusted more than Diana. "OK, but don't tell him I sent you."

I pretended not to see her as she made her way through the crowd to the other end of the bar. While she talked to him, I put an "I know nothing" look on my face (an extremely easy thing for me to do) and casually chair-bopped to the music.

Then I watched, amazed, as the cutie pie climbed off his stool and began to follow Diana back to me.

And this is how it started. Without Diana I would never have had a life ~ which seemed to have begun as soon as we met, in the late 1960s, both of us a couple of years out of high school and waitressing at Bob's Big Boy in the San Fernando Valley. Soon after, we were best friends and sharing an apartment.

We spent most days at the beach. On nights off, we would drive to the Ash Grove on Melrose in West Hollywood to see the Rising Sons ~ or to Ciro's, a nightclub on Sunset Boulevard where we danced to the Byrds (live!) while they played "Bells of Rhymney." We were the idiot girls who sometimes spoke in fake English accents ~ pretending we were visiting America on holiday ~ to any hapless male folk in our vicinity. She was Daphne and I was Muriel. Everywhere we went, all I had to do was point out cute boys and Daphne would go get them for me.

I always wished I could do the same for her, but I just could not bring myself to approach boys. With her blond hair and soulful brown eyes, Diana could do this brave thing and they were putty in her hands.

So in 1971, when Diana decided she wanted to be a nurse like her mother and the school where she'd been accepted was three hours north in a small town called San Luis Obispo, what could I do but go with her? Anyway, I wanted to leave LA, too. It was getting crowded, and this would be a new adventure. San Luis Obispo wasn't far; it would be easy to get back home to see our families and friends.

We talked my brother Jim into filling his pickup with our stuff, and the three of us caravanned up Highway 101, Diana in her black VW filled with boxes of shoes and records, me in my turquoise Corvair, packed with all our thrift store treasures, dishes, and kitchen stuff. Our beds and other furniture were tied to the truck with ropes. We sang along with our eight-tracks,

"...And it's 1-2-3, what're we fightin' for?
Don't ask me I don't give a damn..."

on our way through sun-drenched, geranium-spattered Santa Barbara, up and over the Santa Ynez Mountains, past hillsides of wild lupin and California poppies, to sun-drenched, jacaranda-speckled San Luis Obispo.

25

SLO Town, as everyone called it, was nestled between a chain of long-extinct volcanic peaks called the Nine Sisters. The pleasant, tree-lined downtown was filled with small eclectic businesses centered on a meandering creek and a large adobe mission founded in 1772 by Father Junipero Serra. Because of Cal Poly (the local college), there were lots of cafés, book-stores, live music, and dancing, and SLO was only 10 miles from the beach. Spiced with orange blossoms and eucalyptus trees, San Luis Obispo had barely changed since the 1950s. It was a town that some-day, far in the future, Oprah Winfrey would call

"the happiest city in America."

We lucked into a great apartment on the second floor of an old brick Spanish-style building two blocks from the Mission, within walking distance of everything. It had a long hallway with an arched doorway that opened into a huge living room with a working fireplace and two sets of French doors leading to tiny balconies that hung over the street. We didn't end up using the living room because everything we had, including my sewing machine, fit perfectly in the den next to the kitchen, which was furnished with a farm sink and an old gas stove. The bathroom had a claw-foot tub, and doors from each side into two small bedrooms.

There were small drawbacks to our new apartment, which we hoped the fireplace would make up for. There were no parking places assigned to our building: We had to find parking on the street, which wasn't easy. Groceries had to be carried all the way from the car upstairs to our kitchen, which made getting ice cream home from the market a risky proposition. And there was no washer and dryer ~ pillowcases of dirty laundry had to be carried through the streets to our cars to take to the Laundro-mat. But we were kids and that's how it was.

26

Within two weeks of our arrival, Diana was enrolled in nursing school, and I started my job at Stereo West.

As it turned out, I did get that little kid's spot at the record counter. Danny went back to school, and I got his stool. Elaine was my boss. (Actually Elaine was everyone's boss; not only was she Cliff's right-hand person, she ran the mailroom, accounting, and correspondence departments, too.) My job was to keep the record department organized and alphabet-ized, wait on customers, run the cash register, sell records, and best of all (for me anyway), I was in charge of the music that played throughout the store.

I loved my job from the first. It was like a party every day. The oldest person working at the store was 26, Elaine's husband, Mike, the manager of the sales department. Because everyone was so young, there was lots of flirting, kisses in the storage room, dancing in the mailroom, and constant laughter. We had Cokes across the street at Russell's, lunch on the lawn next to the creek, went shoe shopping on Higuera, and after work we walked down the street to the Cigar Factory for drinks. I would definitely think about what cute thing I was going to wear each day, and in between all that, almost like a sideline to fun, we sold music. It was like "playing store" ~ with no grown-up supervision.

Every so often, Elaine would ask me to work on a special project such as filing or adding names to the mailing list. I also took the deposit to the bank each day, which was about three blocks away, a short walk through town. I got to escape to the sunshine and explore a few shops I passed on my way. My favorite store carried everything for the home; I liked to browse the glass shelves filled with dishes and damask tablecloths. That's where I discovered Beatrix Potter figurines ~ Benjamin Bunny, Jemima Puddleduck, Flopsy, Mopsy, and Cottontail. I wasn't familiar with Beatrix Potter's books, but I took a fancy to these little creatures. They were made in Beswick, England, in the most beautiful colors. I saved money from my paychecks to buy them.

Once Diana was in school and I was working and we were both meeting people, we had no problem adapting to our surroundings. SLO Town was perfectly named: a laid-back small town with hardly any crime, great weather, tons of kids, and lots of live music. On Thursday nights, the stores stayed open late, people would come out, kids cruised, and the downtown was like a street party. On weekends we went to Avila Beach for frozen margaritas and patty melts at the Custom House; we floated down the Salinas River on inner tubes, hiked to the falls at Lopez Lake, walked through the lupin and poppies along the cliffs at Montaña De Oro, and went dancing at Shenandoah or The Graduate.

If we got homesick, we'd drive to LA for the weekend to see our families, singing along with Helen Reddy as we drove down the coast, "YES, I AM WISE, but it's WISDOM BORN of PAIN..."

FLYING BLIND

Despite the emerging women's movement in the early 1970s, I (and most of the girls I knew) had grown up believing we'd fall in love with a wonderful guy and get married in a beautiful dress. Our husbands would work and we'd stay home, keep house, cook dinner, do the laundry, and take care of the children. Our moms were our role models and that's what they did. That belief was deeply ingrained; it was just one of the things I "knew," like my address or that I had hazel eyes.

Around the time I graduated from high school in 1965, two years after the publication of a groundbreaking book I never read called *The Feminine Mystique*, the culture had begun to flip on what seemed to be a dime. Suddenly, my "hope chest" (with all the great stuff in it) looked a little dated. Magazines, books, and TV shows like *That Girl* were telling us to raise our sights, try for more out of life, make our "dreams" come true, stop depending on men to provide for our futures. We should be "independent" and have a "career."

We had not the slightest idea of how to do that. We didn't even really WANT to do it, even though it looked fun on TV. We were just naïve kids, unprepared for the world to change. At the time it all began we were just six years past 12, with one foot trapped in the quicksand of the past and

29

one foot on the slip-'n'-slide of the future. Finding it difficult to understand which way we were supposed to go, we chose the way of the flow, put on miniskirts, tied little leather peace symbols around our necks, and went dancing. We were 18 and we had our priorities.

I should definitely not say "we." I wouldn't want to paint the rest of my generation with my naïveté, I should say "I." I'm sure there were plenty of people on top of these changes just as they were happening, but as a charter member of the baby boom, I could not see the forest for the trees.

By 1971 I was beginning to understand (and even embrace) the reality that we were on the cusp of something new that would require an about-face. But that original belief of traditional family was strong, entrenched from childhood. It was the foundation for all my dreams of life and the only way I'd seen it done.

Me, practicing with two buggies, a crib, a broom, and a six-shooter. Best of all, fashion statement: skirt over pants.

But when a current catches you, there's only one choice: Keep your head up and swim with it.

"...Then you better start swimmin' or you'll sink like a stone, for the times they are a-changin'..."
♥ BOB DYLAN

It was even more confusing for our guys who were brought up just like us: In order to be "real" men, they couldn't be caught dead reading a women's magazine (one of our main sources of information) or books like *Sex and the Single Girl*. They certainly couldn't mouth the words to lyrics like,

"I AM WoMAN WATCH ME GROW. . ."

There were two ducks; the female with the brown head & the other with the green head ~ the unfemale.

♥ DANIELLE RETTINGER – AGE 5

Men were raised to be the head of the family and to be embarrassed if their wives worked, so when we girls started to sing our freedom songs, all they could do was roll their eyes. There was no equivalent of "girl talk" for them. They couldn't listen to females and remain "men," so they suffered from a lack of information, were confused, sometimes angry, and the last to know. I don't think they understood how hard we were being pushed by the culture. I think they thought it was our idea. Our inability to communicate about it caused a huge misunderstanding, which was everyone's loss.

In the 1946 movie *So Goes My Love* with Myrna Loy, the character played by Don Ameche says, "An ambition, Miss Button? Oh, I do hope you're not one of those dreadful girls of the future we're always reading about."

In my heart I was definitely one of the dreadful girls of the future. But I didn't know it yet.

ME & JULIA CHILD

There is wisdom of the head, and ... there is wisdom of the heart. ♥ Charles Dickens

One beautiful day, maybe our second month in town, Diana was studying so I walked over to our landlord's house to pay the rent.

She called, "Come in!" I followed her voice through her house, but I stopped in my tracks when I saw the vision in the dining room.

The table was set for a party. A starched white tablecloth was laid with flowered dishes, gleaming silverware, crystal wine glasses, and bouquets of pink tulips in clear-glass vases. Everything sparkled. I stood there open-mouthed and pop-eyed while tiny fireworks went off in my head. There were even place cards. I'd never seen anything so beautiful.

BEAUTIFUL

I soaked in every detail as I slowly crossed the room to the sunny yellow kitchen ～ filled with the fragrance of cinnamon, onions, rosemary, and garlic mingled with roasting chicken. There was a pie cooling on a wooden rack; the lid rattled and clouds of steam escaped from a large pot on the stove.

WOW DID YOU SEE THAT? I WANT IT!

My landlord was standing barefoot at the counter in front of two windows wide open to a large tree and the garden. She was wearing a sheer white organdy apron over a full pale-pink skirt and a white silk blouse, and was around thirty-two,

32

blond, Grace Kelly-sophisticated, and slicing the biggest, whitest mushrooms I'd ever seen.

Late afternoon sun, warm as a corn muffin, filtered through the windows, throwing leafy splotches of light on the walls, putting gold sparks in her hair, glinting off the glass of white wine on the counter, flashing from the blade of the knife in her hand.

Everything I ever thought I wanted before flew right out the window. Now, all I wanted to be was HER. I took a mental note of every  detail. This wasn't tuna sandwiches she was making. This was entirely different. This was art.

Yes, I thought, my eyes darting from copper pan to wooden spoon, I could do this! Why not? She doesn't own mushrooms. I can get a cute apron like hers. I can make one! She has wine! I like wine!

It was such a pretty picture, home and love and food all mixed together. She was playing house with the real thing!

She wiped her hands on a dishtowel and took my envelope with the rent money; I could see she was busy. I took one last long look at the dining table and left her house with heartstrings loose and flying in total disarray, on a mission. I went directly to the bookstore and bought my first "grown-up" cookbook.

had already been cooking for a long time. My mom taught me to cook when I was a kid. I knew my way around a kitchen, so no one would ever starve. I could make meatloaf, tuna casserole and spaghetti, potato salad, fried chicken, onion dip, brownies, Bisquick pancakes, and almost any kind of cookie. But what I had just seen was different. If I was going to set a table like that (which I had already fully determined I was), I would need something better than tuna casserole to put on it. Up until then, *365 Ways to Cook Hamburger* had been my go-to cookbook. Now I wanted to upgrade.

MASTERING THE ART OF **French** Cooking

The only cookbook that explains how to create authentic French dishes in American kitchens with American foods

BY SIMONE BECK
LOUISETTE BERTHOLLE
JULIA CHILD

Drawings by Sidonie Coryn

browsed the cookbooks at the bookstore and chose *Mastering the Art of French Cooking* by Julia Child. I don't remember why I picked that book. Nothing on it said, "This book will change your life" ~ and it had to be expensive ~ maybe I liked it because it had the word "art" on it. Maybe I'd seen Julia Child cooking on TV, but that's what I came home with. It turned out to be a wonderful decision. Julia Child was in the process of making the world a much better place with her ideas about cooking and entertaining ~ and thanks to the vision of loveliness I'd just experienced (provided by a perfect stranger who never knew what an inspiration she was), I joined the legions of Julia's disciples and did my part to help her change the world, starting with mine.

I think careful cooking is love, don't you? ♥ Julia Child

On my way home from the bookstore, I stopped at the market and bought huge white mushrooms, potatoes, a roasting chicken to go with my new cookbook, and a bouquet of daisies (because from what I'd seen, setting the table was going to be as much fun as cooking) . . . and that was the beginning of my true and forever love for the CREATIVE ART of COOKING.

Diana was my first "victim." I put my new cookbook on the counter and opened it to "Roast Chicken." I said, "Watch this," and poured each of us a glass of wine (so far, she loved it). I turned on the oven, melted some butter, and prepared the chicken following Julia's recipe.

As our kitchen filled with the aroma of roasting chicken, I peeled the potatoes and dropped them into a pan of salted boiling water and sliced those big white mushrooms, which I fried in a dry cast-iron pan until all the juice evaporated and they became crisp. (Fried mushrooms was my own addition; I didn't know what my landlord was going to do with her mushrooms, but the picture would not be complete ∼ I could not be "Her" ∼ unless I sliced mushrooms.) I tore up lettuce for a salad and covered it with the chewy crisp mushrooms.

In between chicken basting, mushroom frying, and sauce making, I brought a votive candle from the coffee table and lit it, then set the table with our meager collection of mismatched dishes. I put the daisies in a jelly jar and folded some paper napkins.

When we cut into that juicy, golden brown, crisp-skinned heavenly bird, and sopped up those tender pieces of potato in butter and gravy and salt and pepper, Diana's big eyes, small round of applause, and words "I think I'm in love" were all I needed to hear. I almost cried. I pushed the cookbook toward her eagerly, "What shall we have tomorrow?" I asked.

TILL THIS MOMENT I
NEVER KNEW MYSELF.

Jane Austen

CHAPTER THREE

I like-a you, you like-a me

NOW IT HAPPENED THAT A PRINCE CAME TO THE FOREST ONE DAY
& WHEN HE ARRIVED AT THE DWARFS' COTTAGE,
HE DECIDED TO SPEND THE NIGHT. ♥ Grimm's Fairy Tales

Six months after I started working for him, Cliff surprised me, coming up behind me just as I turned to hang up the phone. I was sitting on a high swivel stool, sorting photos by event and subject for Elaine, bopping in my seat in my wonderful record department, while Ringo sang "It Don't Come Easy." I thought I felt something on my neck; I turned fast at the surprise of it and we almost bumped heads.

I drew back quickly and right away he said, "Hi. Sue. How's it going?

I was surprised he remembered my name. This was the first time in all those months he had spoken to me directly. Cliff always ran by me, tearing in and out the front door, roaring off in his car, always in a hurry, a man on a mission, hitching up his pants as he went, wearing still another T-shirt from his impressive collection. He never stopped to say hello ⁓ which was fine with me, because, as you can imagine, he made me nervous.

Sometimes he would walk by in serious conversation with the "suits" from the bank, or laughing with his lawyer, or with Tom and sales reps from Bose or Harman Kardon or with his gorgeous blond girlfriend who stopped in to see him a couple of times a week. When he had something on his mind, he'd look right through the employees. He didn't socialize with us. He never came to the Cigar Factory, and we never saw him outside the office.

Elaine talked about both Cliff and Tom a lot ~ she thought they were brilliant, their fingers "on the pulse of the generation" ~ but she worried about the way they tore around in fast cars and on motorcycles. A group of us from work were at the Cigar Factory one night, and one of the guys joked about an idea he had for a get-rich-quick scheme: We should chip in and take out life insurance policies on our bosses because the way they were going, it wouldn't be long 'til the big payoff.

The only time I ever saw Cliff and Tom together and up close was at our regular Thursday night employee meetings after work. The two of them were intense, excited, passionate, and hard-working. The store was anything but a game to them; they were determined to be a success. At 22, Tom was just as wild as Cliff, they both loved motorcycles and hot cars, but Tom was quieter; Cliff called him the brains of the operation. But Cliff did most of the talking. He had a vision, and his enthusiasm was infectious; we believed in him, we believed in them. The town believed in them, the newspaper wrote about them, and the bank loaned

Tom & Cliff ~ & Elaine ~
the true brains of the operation. ♡

38

them money. Cliff was different; we were all goldfish swimming with the current, but he was a giant squid, self-propelled, reaching in all directions. We loved our jobs because of him, because we felt like we'd hitched our wagons to a star ～ a squid star.

Fine. I'm fine," I said to his question of how I was doing. But I was startled and a little worried because of the sudden attention. What does he want? While this guy was out conquering the world, I was home em-broidering butterflies on my jeans.

"How's the job going?" he asked.

"Pretty good, as far as I know." I'm wondering if I did something wrong.

"That's good to hear. Elaine says you caught on fast. Did she tell you you're the first person we've hired from a newspaper ad?"

"I did hear that. Pretty amazing ～ you always hired friends before me. Guess I was in the right place. Ha ha." Why am I laughing?

"Yeah, you were ～ we thought it was time to bring in some new blood. Glad it's working out."

I nodded, "Yes, well, thank you." (Now please go away.)

I was about to turn back to my work when he added, "You know, I should have welcomed you more officially. Taken you to lunch. How about tomorrow?"

"OK," I said. Yikes, I thought. Do I have to?

"OK, far out, noon. I'll come get you right here."

And that was that. He took off, tearing out the door, hitching up his pants as he went. (I had begun to think the pants hitching was his way of keeping track of things. Why didn't he wear a belt?)

Suddenly I was going to lunch with my maniac boss. I'd be alone with him in his car. What would we talk about? The rest of the afternoon I worried. Seems so strange out of the blue like this. What does he want? What shall I wear?

Later that night at home, while grating potatoes for Julia's Crepes de Pommes de Terre, I mentioned Cliff's invitation to Diana.

"Who?"

"You know, my boss, Cliff."

"Oh yeah, the guy with the Velcro. Why's he taking you to lunch?" She opened the fridge, staring into it mindlessly. "He's pretty cute. Is this a date?" She looked over at me.

"Get out of there, I'm making something you're going to love, don't eat anything now. And no, it's definitely NOT a date, he's my boss and he has a girlfriend. I think he's just being nice, sort of like Welcome Wagon. I'm not sure. I hope he isn't going to fire me or something."

"I don't think people take people to lunch to fire them. What are you going to wear?"

"That's what I was wondering. I don't know, I think the jean skirt I've been working on. It's finished. Wait til you see ∿ I even put eyelet on the hem. It's supposed to be nice tomorrow. Can I borrow your platforms?"

At noon the next day Cliff came by my desk, jangled his car keys at me, and asked, "Ready to go?" I was nervous as we climbed into his little blue convertible ∿ not really nervous because of him, but more because he was my boss and always in such a rush. What would I say, what could we have in common? Not dirt bikes. I was afraid I would bore him ∿ I didn't see how he could sit still for an entire lunch.

He drove to the restaurant at a small adobe hotel on the edge of town.

Motel Inn was built in the 1920s and made famous when Marilyn Monroe and Joe DiMaggio stopped there for lunch while on their honeymoon in 1954. The restaurant was on a patio in a garden next to a sparkling turquoise swimming pool surrounded with hedges of bottlebrush and purple flowering jacaranda trees. Baskets of fuchsias hung from the porch roof, and lots of hummingbirds zipped in and out.

I ordered a club sandwich with potato salad. Cliff had a cheeseburger and fries. We both got Cokes.

"So," he leaned back in his chair with a little smile and leveled his blue eyes at me, "you just moved here, right?"

"Yeah, about six months ago," I said, twisting the straw paper around my finger, "like a week before I started at Stereo West."

"From down south?"

"Yeah, the Valley."

Hmmmm?

He asked if I'd moved to SLO alone, and I told him I'd come with my best friend, Diana.

"Oh, I think I've seen her with you. Is she the blond? *(He's seen her with me!)* So, what do you think so far, how do you like it here?" It made me squirm the way he fixed his eyes on me.

"San Luis? I really like it. The Valley has gotten so crowded, too much traffic ~ I felt like I was standing in line for everything." I was getting more uncomfortable. Get *this* off me, I thought. "Did you grow up here?"

"I grew up in Carmel Valley, moved to Santa Barbara when I was 15 ~ then up here when I was 18 to go to Cal Poly."

42

The conversation got easier, especially when he did most of the talking. We got a little used to each other, and pretty soon he was telling me about the accident where he broke his shoulder and how he and Tom met at Cal Poly, and how they started their business.

He was excited about an old brick warehouse they were thinking of buying for the mail-order part of the company. He talked about ads he was doing for Playboy and Rolling Stone.

Cliff was passionate when he talked about business ～ he was sick of mainstream "plastic" and said what kids wanted was authenticity in products that performed as promised, but also he thought that what went on behind the scenes should have integrity. He laughed when he said, "I'm not a Republican or a Democrat, my party is rock and roll." He believed music would change the world. He was idealistic and brimming with self-confidence ～ nothing was going to slow him down.

You couldn't not like him; I never heard anyone talk like that before. Only 21 with dreams about changing the world ～ and he wasn't afraid to talk about them. Wow is what I thought. Did he talk to every girl like this? Because I felt like having this cute guy tell me what was in his heart was a huge compliment, like I was getting a gold star. I was flattered by the attention from this positive person who inspired such admiration from everyone I knew.

He seemed in no hurry to get back to the office. It was such a gorgeous day there by the pool. I was having fun and figured I couldn't get into too much trouble with Elaine since I was with the boss. I heard all about his girlfriend, Bonnie ~ they met at a stoplight driving downtown ~ that was original ~ not too many people meet at stoplights. He said she was really sweet, but too young (she was 18, going to Cal Poly, and he was an old man at 21) and how it was a "relationship of convenience," whatever that was.

"Know why I hired you?" he asked.

"No. Why?"

"Because you remind me of me."

"Of you?"

"Yeah, you were so impatient to know if you got the job you practically ordered me to tell you immediately. You wouldn't even give me 24 hours."

"I was just excited. I needed the job ~ and it looked like fun."

"Yeah, I know, and I thought, This girl has guts, she's intelligent, she sticks up for what she wants. That's why I hired you. Any girl that sure of herself deserved the job."

He thought I had guts. He thought I was confident. Obviously, he was unaware of the clammy-hand syndrome I was experiencing at that very moment. I was surprised, but as long as he liked that kind of thing, I was glad I was the one who did it. (I tried to impress him like this many times in the future. It didn't always go as well as it did the first time.)

We spent two hours talking and laughing about everything under the sun. On the way back to work, going too fast under the trees with the top down and the music up, the wind in my face and all of San Luis Obispo in the air, I felt free and young and happy. Tom Jones sang,

"...WELL, SHE'S ALL YOU'D EVER WANT, SHE'S THE KIND YOU'D LIKE TO FLAUNT & TAKE TO DIN-NER..."

About a week later Elaine gave me directions to Cliff's house and sent me over with an armful of files to deliver. It was a small ranch-style house in a neighborhood up behind the college where he'd lived since he moved to SLO to go to school.

He opened the door like he'd been waiting for me and said, "Hi! Hey, come here," taking the files and putting them on a table. "I want you to hear something."

I followed him into the living room ～ he leaned over a turntable and dropped a record over the spindle, moved the stylus into the groove, and turned up the volume before it even started to play.

He playfully pulled me next to him in a large black-leather swivel chair close to the stereo, saying, "You need to sit here to get the full effect."

Uh huh, I thought. Of course I wanted the "full effect," but this seemed like trouble.

We were faced straight into a pair of floor speakers, maybe six feet in front of us. I moved forward a little bit and he shifted, which brought me back. I thought about getting up, but I was

45

afraid it would be weird, so I acted like it was natural. I liked him, but I also worked for him.

I stayed kind of squashed in next to him and listened as the music started, "She packed my bags last night preflight . . ." The piano was strong and lyrical, and Elton John's familiar voice sang, ". . . he missed his wife, it's lonely out in space . . ." The piano keys pounded and started to climb, and then, BOOM, a guitar riff joined the piano and together they flew the music right up to the sky and me right along with it:
    ". . . and I think it's gonna be a long long time . . ."
Rifffff, the chorus taking me even higher.
    Cliff leaned over and turned up the volume,
        ". . . Rocket Ma – a – an . . ."
            It was the best song I'd ever heard.

And then it ended. I came back to earth and my thoughts started tumbling. I'm only here to drop off papers. What am I doing? Cliff was cute and fun to be with, but he was my boss and he had a girlfriend. I had to get back. Elaine was waiting. Even worse, what if Bonnie came in?

Before I could move, Cliff got up, leaving me in the chair. I started to get up, too.

"Wait," he said, "you have to hear this!" He pushed a button on the stereo and plunked headphones on my head. Big, black, soft headphones. Now I was actually inside the music. I sat there, alone in the big leather chair, swinging back and forth.

I couldn't hear anything but the music. Cliff was across the room at a chrome and glass dining table fooling around with the papers I'd brought. I felt a little self-conscious, I was sort of in a stranger's house, so I closed my eyes to listen (because this was what he wanted me to do) ～ it was a brand new song, just out,

♪ "*Wake up, Maggie, I think I have something to say to you...*" ♥ *Rod Stewart*

My eyes were only closed for a moment, and when I opened them, Bonnie, was standing there looking at me, blinking, then over at him. Her arms were full of books, and I'm sure she was wondering what this person was doing in her house with her boyfriend when she wasn't home. It was a good question.

I jumped up and took off the headphones while Cliff reminded her who I was. I said hello. Then, making my excuses, I got out the front door as fast as I could, with Cliff following behind me, laughing, "You don't have to go. She won't mind. Stay."

I turned, walking backward toward my car, and said, "I really can't. Elaine told me to come right back ～ I need to get going." I didn't want to be in the middle of whatever this was.

Later on at home, while slicing an avocado onto a toasted English muffin, I told Diana what happened.

"He's cute, Diana, but he's definitely trouble. I think he must like me, otherwise why would he practically put me on his lap?"

"Are you kidding? He's a guy. He doesn't have to like you. Doesn't he have a girlfriend? Can I have a bite of that?"

Me, apparently practicing for
a mug shot.

"I made you half ~ and yes, that's what I mean by trouble. She came in while I was there."

"What's she like?"

"I wasn't there long enough to find out When we went to lunch he told me they met at a stoplight on Higuera. She wears hot pants into the store. She looks like a Playboy bunny ~ tall, tan, gorgeous, long blond hair, 18. I don't know what he's thinking, having me come over there."

"Hot pants. God. I wonder if she was wearing them at the stoplight? He's probably thinking how nice it is to get you to bring him things. So now what?" she asked.

"Now, nothing." I said, laughing at her. "I'm staying away from him. He probably does this music thing in the chair with everyone. And, he's my boss."

The only problem with "now, nothing" was that I had to go to work every day.

And from then on, Cliff was friendly ~ very cute and flirty and I stopped feeling so tongue-tied around him. I felt like we were becoming friends. Nothing else, really ~ he kept his distance, I never saw him after hours. Then after a week or two, he began (as I explained it to Diana) to make me his "real estate buddy."

"Doing anything for lunch today?" he'd say, screeching to a stop at the record counter.

"Not really," I'd laugh.

"I need to go over to the warehouse building ～ you want to come with me? We'll get sandwiches at Gus's Grocery."

"OK," I'd say, "but you'll bring me back in an hour? Right? I don't want Elaine mad at me."

He told me not to worry, he knew the boss, he could even make it part of my job to go look at real estate with him.

Which is basically what he did . . . A couple of times a week we would jump into his car, turn up the music, and drive somewhere ～ over the grade to look at a trout farm he was interested in, up the coast to Cambria to look at a piece of land, or out to Pismo Beach to see a house. It definitely made life interesting ～ it was FUN to go to work. There was nothing going on (I'd say to myself when Bonnie popped into my head). Cliff and I were just friends. Bonnie was at school, and I was handy. It was all very exciting. I probably had a crush on him and didn't even know it.

We ate takeout cheeseburgers and Cokes as we drove to wherever he wanted to go. I got to know him a little bit. I heard about his family, his parents. I learned he was student body president in high school. He told me he wrote a book, a novel, when he was 17. It wasn't published, but I was impressed he'd even tried. I never saw him outside work, no "dates," it wasn't like that.

He was in perpetual motion, looking at real estate, running his business, and racing his dirt bike. He wasn't social in the same way as my other friends. He didn't party. He told me about his five-year plan. It was all about business and cars, but I'd never heard of anyone having a five-year plan. (No one I knew had a five-day plan.)

A few weeks later, it was Diana's birthday, and she and I decided to have our first big party. Our huge, almost-empty living room with the polished wood floors was perfect for dancing. We invited everyone we knew, including Cliff and Bonnie ~ but we knew they wouldn't come. We never saw them out anywhere.

We made a big cake, sandwiches, guacamole, and bought lots of chips . It was BYOB. We lit candles and cranked the music. I wore a zip-up-the-front lavender-flowered jumpsuit with wide, flowing bell bottoms, three-inch slip-on Candies, and lavender granny glasses. Diana had on a green Mexican lace skirt with matching off-the-shoulder embroidered blouse and her platform sandals with fruit on them. As usual, we had as much fun putting on our makeup, making faces in the mirror, trying on clothes and getting dressed as we did at the party.

Candies

High heels were invented by a woman who'd been kissed on the forehead.
♥ Christopher Morley

The noise levels picked up. Everyone was dancing, standing on the balconies, drinking beer, leaning on counters in the kitchen, crowding the dark, smoky hallway, maybe fifty or sixty people. Somewhere around midnight, I was downstairs at the front door saying good-bye to friends when Cliff stepped out of the shadows. By himself. *That's funny ~ how long has he been there?* And he wouldn't come up; he wanted me to come outside. I stood in the doorway telling him, "No, I can't go. We're having a party, in case you didn't notice."

But he wouldn't be put off. Smiling impishly and saying, "Come with me," he reached in, grabbed my arm, and pulled me toward him. I pushed back, my hand on his chest, but he pulled harder and then he had me ~ he picked me up in his arms and started down the street! I wanted to be angry, but (a) I kind of liked it and (b) I was laughing so hard, he knew I kind of liked it.

The top was down on his car, and he put me into the front seat. I acted mad and told him this was going on his permanent record, but he didn't care. He turned up the music and drove out to Avila Beach, under the stars, the back way. I was telling him about the party, who was there ~ and on a dark curve in the road he pulled over, stopped the car, reached across the console, took me by my shoulders, pulled me close, said, "I like having you around" and kissed me on the lips.

I didn't even close my eyes ~ I was too surprised. He liked having me around! "What are you doing?" I asked, thinking out loud. In response, he pulled me back and kissed me again, and this time I kissed him back. And that's when I knew things had changed between us. I was confused, a little scared, and suddenly half in love. With crickets chirping and balmy nighttime all around us, it didn't feel real. We got back onto the highway, the top was down, the moon was shining, the windows were up, the heat was on, he drove fast, we didn't talk, just listened to Elton:

"Blue jean baby, LA lady, seamstress for the band..."

51

The wind is rushing after us,
& the clouds are flying after us,
and the moon is plunging after us,
& the whole wild night is in pursuit of us.

CHARLES DICKENS

It was late, and when I asked him, he took me home. The next day, while in the kitchen sweeping up cigarette ashes and potato-chip crumbs, I wondered if I had dreamed the whole thing. Could this be love? I sure hoped so. It was Sunday but I didn't hear from him all day. I imagined he was with Bonnie. It didn't feel good.

On Monday, Cliff and Tom flew to Chicago for the Consumer Electronics Show. They were going to be gone a week. I saw Bonnie in town, so I knew he didn't take her. I felt much better.

I worked hard to talk myself out of the fantasies that popped into my head, and by the end of the week I was back to my calm, normal self, making curtains for our kitchen and going out dancing with Diana, definitely not in love with my boss.

The day he got back, I was at work, sitting on a step stool in the basement at the end of a long row of gray metal shelves stacked with stereo boxes, packing up styluses to take upstairs to the sales department. I heard someone clattering down the stairs and looked up to see who it was. Cliff was bounding toward me like a St. Bernard puppy.

"**H**iiiiii!" he said, not slowing down. I kind of scrambled to my feet because he looked like he might gallop right into me. In one motion he came to a stop, twirled me around, and kissed me long and hard, a real kiss ∼ he smelled like soap and I melted into him like a rag doll. When he let me up for air (which took a while, I'm happy to say, because I lived off that kiss for years), I had the presence of mind to croak, "Hey, what's going on?" My sole claim to consciousness.

"Bonnie moved out," he beamed. "I asked her to go before I left and she did. She moved in with her girlfriend while I was in Chicago."

I was shocked. Pent-up uncertainty was draining away and hope jumped into its place. I didn't know what to say. He broke up with *her* (as it was looking) for me? Bonnie's long brown legs flashed through my mind. "Really?" I repeated, "she moved out?" I couldn't believe it.

"Really," he said.

"And that's why you're here?" I asked, my heart doing back flips.

"What do you think?" he said, his arms wrapped around me, looking into my eyes with his cute Jeff Bridges ripply hair falling over his forehead. I tried to answer, but his lips got in the way.

Diana wasn't so sure. She thought that being with Cliff was playing with fire. I had to agree. I was the moth and he was the flame.

When Roberta Flack sang *Killing Me Softly with His Song*, I sang every word right along with her.

The thing was, this young boy with massive charm just kept coming after me, stealing my heart, making me feel special, seeing something in me I didn't know I had, changing my world, to the point where I could not refuse, and really, why would I?

At the side of the everlasting why, is a yes, and a yes, and a yes. ♥ E. M. Forster

People at work had already noticed me and Cliff and our "adventures" in real estate, but now it went to a whole new level. At our Thursday night company meetings he made eyes at me, flirted, and stared until I had to look away, shaking my head, embarrassed by the attention. People at the meeting were like the audience at Wimbledon. Eyes to me, then to him, back to me, back to him. He didn't care. He was having fun. I mouthed the word "STOP." He didn't stop. He was a maniac.

"Moons and tunes and ferris wheels, the dizzy dancing ♪ way you feel, as every fairy tale comes true...." ♫ ♥ Joni Mitchell

He left notes in my car, flowers under the windshield wiper. I met his parents. We went to Tom's, and I met Tom's parents, too. We went to dinner with his best friends: his builder

friend, John, and his wife, Carol; his lawyer friend, Jim, and his girlfriend, Beverly; his doctor friend, Ben, and his wife, Pat; his printer friend, Dick, and his dog, Stink the Wonder Dog. Cliff's friends became my friends too. ♥

We went for long drives up the coast and snuggled while we watched the sun set from the bluffs at Montaña de Oro. In Avila we ran across the street from the waves and the sand to Barbara's by the Sea, a funky old beach bar that smelled like a thousand wet bathing suits, where we drank chocolate shakes while entwining sandy toes on the cold cement floor under the table. He was always dropping headphones over my ears for a song he thought I'd like. After work on Thursdays, we'd walk through town, slipping into dark doorways for passionate kisses. My diary was ON fire!

"I thought love was only true in fairy tales, meant for someone else but not for me..."
The Monkees

I think I actually saw the exact moment Cliff fell in love with me. Late one night, we were talking. I don't remember how it started, but he was saying he thought I had too much of a fairy tale view of the world. I should be aware that it wasn't always roses.

DO NOT DISTURB

I turned my face up and asked him, because I really wanted to know, "Can't we just make things the way we want them to be? Isn't life like a choice? Like you decide what's going to happen and then you just make it that way?"

I saw his blue eyes melt, a little smile played on his lips, and butterflies fluttered in my tummy. I don't know if he thought the question was naïve, or if he saw some sort of truth in it, or if he just liked the optimism it conveyed; but whatever it was, his face turned to love. He put his arm around my waist and pulled me to him, his lips fell on my neck, and he said, very softly, "Fairy tale girl." And that's exactly how I felt, like I was living in a fairy tale.

When we were at the movies, instead of looking at the screen, he would watch me watch the movie.

...You take a lover who looks at you like maybe you are magic.
Frida Kahlo

I loved cooking for him ~ cooking was like my secret weapon. We weren't living together, but that didn't stop me from going into classic nesting mode. I brought my favorite cookbook to his house and made Julia's French omelet. I slid the little soft thing onto his plate. He took one bite, looked up with a mouthful of buttery goodness, and said, "How'd you learn to do that?"

I broiled steaks, pink and juicy; I buttered and salted the skin of a potato before I put it into the oven so it would bake crisp and crunchy and smoking hot.

It was all over but the mopping up when I made Coq au Vin. When I spooned the long-simmering chicken and wine sauce onto his plate, and snuggled it with the sinfully delicious browned and braised baby onions along with the sautéed mushrooms, his eyes rolled. I licked a drip of sauce off the side of his mouth and said a silent prayer, THANK YOU, JULIA ♥

"...Well, I walked to my house like a good girl should, he followed me to my house like I knew he would..."
♥ Doris Day

"Cookies!" Cliff said, his eyes flashing around the kitchen, "It smells like cookies in here! Where are they?"
"What? I don't have cook---" ♥
He interrupted, "You do too, I smell them! Where are they?"
"I don't, I don't . . ." I was leaning against the counter wearing his Led Zeppelin T-shirt, and he started trying to find cookies in the ❧ pockets of my jeans, patting me down like I was a prisoner. He turned me around to check my back pockets and I was laughing and although he never found any cookies, no one cared. Next time, I thought, I will salt myself in cookies.

Tonight. Same time. Same place.

He dropped the headphones on me, Leon Russell sang in his craggy splintered voice

"...I love you in a place where there's no space or time..." ♪

We were getting no sleep. I still lived with Diana; she and I still did things together. I got up and went to work every day, and there he was, and there I was, trying not to give myself away too much, the head-over-heelsness of the situation, the wild imaginary future I was conjuring up for us.

And then I did the thing:

I wrote
"Susan Branch"
in my diary

and
"Mrs. Cliff Branch"

Do you believe
in rock & roll?
Can music save
your mortal soul?
And can you teach me
how to dance real slow?
Don McLean

CHAPTER FOUR

DOMESTIC BLISS

Allerleirauh made the soup for the king, the best she could, and when it was ready she fetched her golden ring from her little den, kissed it and dropped it in the bowl in which the soup was served.
♥ Brothers Grimm

Diana and I decided to cook our first Thanksgiving dinner at our apartment and make it a party. We invited Cliff and his parents; Paul, a friend of Cliff's (and the guy Diana was dating); Lorrie, a girlfriend from work; Elaine and Mike; Cliff's two brothers, Tony and Greg; and Greg's wife, Jenny. Twelve.

Our mostly empty living room ran the full width of the apartment; there was a Mexican-tiled fireplace at one end and a heavy, Mexican-style dining table that came with the apartment at the other. It was the perfect spot for Thanksgiving. We shoved the table in front of the fireplace and bought some firewood.

None of our dishes matched and we had to borrow plates from Elaine, but it didn't matter. I starched and ironed an old tablecloth my mom gave me, along with a set of white damask napkins I'd found in an antique store shortly after Julia Child came into my life. Only 25 cents each, and I already knew I would want them for all the Thanksgivings of my life.

I spread the cloth on the table. Only one tiny hole ~ I put a vase of flowers over it. We had matching wine glasses (not jelly jars) ~ I splurged and got them for 59 cents each at the local department store. Everybody got a knife and fork. It was very civilized, considering I had never made a whole dinner for this many people. How hard could it be? I thought. My mom cooked Thanksgiving for at least 12 of us every year.

So I did it just the way she and grandma did it Nothing came from Julia's book. This was a pure homemade old-fashioned holiday family dinner, the same one served in almost every house in America: turkey, stuffing, mashed potatoes, gravy, cranberry sauce. Soul food.

It was my first time cooking a turkey by myself. It was a big one, 17 pounds, and when I rinsed it I found something scary in the cavity. To be on the safe side, not wishing to touch it (we must remember, I was 24), I wrapped  my hand in a dishcloth, reached in, pulled the thing out and threw it in the trash. (My mom wasn't home when I called, but later she told me it was the neck.) I patted the turkey dry, and Diana and I wrestled it into the pan. We stuffed it with my grandma's stuffing, slathered the skin with melted butter, surrounded it with peeled carrots and chopped onions to flavor the juices, and basted it until it was brown and crisp.

When everyone arrived, Frank Sinatra was on the stereo singing "Fly Me to the Moon," and the apartment was filled with the fragrance of sage and butter, cinnamon and apples, pumpkin and baking biscuits. Logs were burning brightly in the fireplace, the French doors to the little balconies were open, candles were lit, and flowers were on the table. There was a choice of wine: Blue Nun or Mateus (we had recently graduated from our Boone's Farm phase ～ lucky for everyone, it was getting quite sophisticated in our household by then).

We held hands, and I recited the hymn my grandma used to say for our Thanksgiving prayer:

For the beauty of the earth,
For the glory of the skies,
For the love which from our birth
Over and around us lies ～
Lord of all, to thee we raise
This our hymn of grateful praise.

We raised our glasses and Cliff's dad added, "To absent friends." "To absent friends," we echoed. We ♫ clicked our glasses, and the bells of friendship rang.

I didn't burn anything, it was all hot at the same time, no one said, "Eeeew." It was a total success.

61

e took turns feeding Elaine's dog, Boxcar, under the table: slivers of turkey, dough balls of dressing. Cliff's mom, Betty, was so complimentary. When she broke open a biscuit and the steam came rolling out, she looked at me and I felt like I could see little hearts coming out of her eyes toward me. Hearts were going in both directions, from my eyes to hers, too.

She kept marveling how we were so young to have made this big dinner. "How did you learn to do this?" she asked. "Tell me about your family." From this night forward, Betty was always like this with me ~ a wonderfully-supportive, brilliant, life-loving role model of a woman who called me "Susie."

Russ & Betty

Cliff's dad, Russ, leaned toward me while drowning his plate in gravy and said, "Don't tell Betty, but this is the best dressing I ever tasted." He liked my grandma's stuffing (I fell in love with him; who could not love someone who loved your grandma's stuffing?).

veryone asked for more of everything. The bowls and platters kept going around the table, glasses were refilled, the fire crackled, a breeze fluttered the curtains, more toasts were made, and I was in heaven.

I was happy because they were happy. And Cliff? He was proud. It was something new, feeding parents instead of the other way around. He watched his mom and dad, and he watched me. Honestly, I really think this dinner sealed the deal (as much as this deal was sealable, that is).

O nly one small glitch, and it happened after everyone was gone and we were cleaning up. I was picking the rest of the meat off the carcass, and that's when I found a tiny paper bag hidden in a little pouchlike cavity on the front of the turkey.

"Hey, look at this." I held it up to show Diana.

"What is it?" she said.

"That's what I was going to ask you. It's a bag." ~ I cautiously tore it open and peered in. "It looks like liver."

"Oh! I bet it's the giblets, the liver and the guts."

"What's it doing in here?"

"I don't know. They give them to you. Comes with the turkey. Probably his heart, too. Let me look."

I emptied the bag onto a plate and Nurse Diana probed the dried-out contents with the pick-up stick I used as a cake tester.

GIBLET ALERT

Remove from turkey, delicious to flavor gravy.

" Yup, there's the heart all right. I don't think you were supposed to leave this inside when you cooked it."

"Well, I don't think so either. Why didn't they put a little flag on it or something? It's like they hid it. I'll call my mom tomorrow and ask her what I was supposed to do with this. I'm sure we weren't supposed to eat it. Can you imagine what Cliff's mom would have thought if this little bag of guts had plopped out on her plate? I would have died."

Diana laughed until she had to run for the bathroom.

This was my first dinner party. I learned that it didn't matter what the table looked like ～ whether my dishes matched or if there was a hole in the tablecloth. Make a dinner ～ something old-fashioned and delicious that reminds everyone of their childhood ～ turn off all the lights, put a vase of flowers over the hole in the tablecloth, light a lot of candles, pass the wine, and let the faces of friends and loved ones make the table shine.

Cooking and setting a pretty table made me feel like I had something to give, something that made life a little sweeter for other people, so that every day wouldn't be like every other. All that in a little thing like cooking.

But I was a pure romantic & operating with only half my burners turned on. ♥ Julia Child

Nesting 1972～3

One day Cliff pulled up in front of the store in his brand-new white Pantera. I heard the car first, and through the front windows I saw him jump out and come rushing through the door and over to my desk.

He grabbed my arm and said, "Come on, let's go, I have something to show you. Get in the car."

"Right now?" I was scrambling off my stool.

"Yes! Now! Get in the car."

He was excited and tugging me toward the door; I looked back helplessly at Elaine, who smiled and shook her head. Laughing and shrugging my shoulders, I got in the car ～ and away we roared.

"Listen," he said, turning up the volume on the stereo.

"Doctor, my eyes have seen the years
and the slow parade of fears . . ."

"Who is it?" I asked.

"It's a new guy named Jackson Browne." And onto the freeway we zoomed, heading south.

Cliff had just put a deposit on a new house and he wanted to show it to me. This was the first I'd heard of it, I didn't even know he was looking for a house. We drove down a sandy little street close to the beach and into the driveway of a redwood house perched on the side of a hill. It had an almost all-glass front, a wraparound deck, and a small Mexican-tiled swimming pool. Surrounded by palm trees and ferns, birds of paradise and lavender, the house looked out over the tiled rooftops of Shell

Beach, to the wide curve of coastline maybe a quarter mile away with a view of the whole wide spar-kling sea all the way to Pismo, past the Oceano Dunes to Guadalupe.

I followed Cliff through the empty rooms, thinking, *The bed goes there, the dresser goes there.* While he examined the hot water heater and the electrical panel, I walked out to the garden to put

my nose in the angel's trumpet, then around to the back deck to look at the water and watch the seagulls drift over the surf.

There was something about all of it that made me feel alone. The day was achingly perfect, with the sky and the smell of the ocean and the seagulls crying. So beautiful and, in my frame of mind, so sad. I wanted Cliff to ask me to move in with him. But he didn't even tell me he was buying a house. He obviously wasn't including me. My heart ached. I loved him so much, but I could see he didn't love me. I was a mass of tearful (and very likely, hormonal) confusion.

I wished desperately to be part of his five-year plan. Probably, I thought, tears brimming over as I envisioned my tragic future, he'll live in this beautiful house with some other girl, and I'll go away sad and broken-hearted, never find love, never marry, just wither away until I'm dead.

I had worked myself into a state of pathetic, unfulfilled yearnings ~ abandoned by the whole world when Cliff came up behind me and wrapped his arms around me. We stood quietly, swaying a bit in the breeze, looking out at the wide blue sea ~ I was glad he couldn't see my tears. He pulled me closer, and with his mouth against my hair he said, "Come live here with me."

My heart stopped. "What?" I whirled around, not caring if he saw I was crying because new tears were coming, and they were from happiness. "Really? You really want to? You didn't even tell me you were looking for a house."

"I know. I wanted to surprise you. Do you like it?"

It was like going from zero to 60 in less than three seconds. I threw my arms around him and kissed him with the biggest exclamation point of a kiss I could. "I love it! I love you! Yes, yes, yes!" And then I skipped into the kitchen and turned on and off all the burners and the faucets, opened and closed the fridge, trying everything on for size, thinking, *The table will go there, and my Beatrix Potter people will fit perfectly on that window sill,* with the happiest heart ever known to womankind.

Of course, the first person I told was Diana. It was OK with her, sort of. Actually it was a little hard on both of us. We had so much fun together for such a long time. But she had fallen madly in love with an architect friend of Cliff's who taught at Cal Poly; they'd been talking about moving in together for weeks. The timing couldn't have been better. We were getting older, twenty-five now. It was time to settle down.

We hashed it over in Diana's black VW, on the way to our favorite spot on Avila Beach, next to the pier, past the first lifeguard stand.

Diana, rubbing baby oil on her legs, looked at me: "Are we crazy moving in with these guys? Giving up our apartment to go live with them?"

I was arranging my towel, getting my diary out of my bag. "Probably, but really, what's going to be different. We're always with them anyway."

" Yeah, but now we'll have to be with them. There'll be no place to hide." She was getting comfy with her book, leaning against her striped canvas backrest. "Pretty soon you'll get married, then I'll get married, we'll have babies and get busy, and we'll drift apart."

I rolled onto my tummy and looked up at her. "No, we won't. That's not going to happen. We'll never drift apart. We're friends for life. You have a girl baby, I'll have a boy. We'll take them to the park, take them to the beach, they'll grow up, fall in love and get married, and we'll be related and together forever. Think of their wedding!!!"

"Ooooh, I can't wait!"

Cliff wanted me to quit my job ∼ which made sense to me, too. For all practical purposes I hadn't been much good to Stereo West for quite a while ∼ long weekends, lunches, late arrivals, early departures, and days off had become more frequent due to whims and desires of the boss (and the employee). Elaine would not miss me at work. I'd become more trouble than I was worth ～ she needed actual workers she could depend on. She and I were now friends for life anyway.

Elaine and Cliff

So we all got together and decided to fire me.

Cliff helped me move my stuff out of the apartment and into the Shell Beach house to take up my new and improved position as his full-time girlfriend.

We drove up the coast via Big Sur to San Francisco to shop together for the house. Cliff said I could get whatever we needed for the kitchen; I'd felt like I won the lottery. I got Cuisinart pots and pans with wooden handles, nesting bowls, sharp knives, a pig-shaped cutting board, wooden spoons, and wire whisks.

He chose the furniture: chrome-and-glass-topped tables, large colorful stalactite specimens (as bookshelf décor), Plexiglas chairs, leather pillows, and a leather sofa.

Stalactite
Specimens

"No coffee table?" I asked. "No," he said. He did not "believe in" coffee tables. (I did not believe in leather sofas or stalactite specimens, but I was not in charge.)

I was not complaining, not even a little bit, it was all fun ～ and also, for the first time since I'd moved away from my parents' home, I didn't have to go sit around the depressing

Laundromat waiting for my clothes to dry. There was a washer and dryer in the house! It was beyond my wildest dreams. It marked my true entry into adulthood. The only people I knew who had their own washer and dryer were grownups. My mom didn't get a clothes dryer until I was around 11. She got it for Christmas and just about went crazy with happiness, screamed when she saw it in the garage, sat down, and cried from joy. I felt the same way.

I phased out Cliff's brown and black striped sheets and bought new ones with little blue flowers on them. We slept with the sliding door open, made love under the lightest of feathery down comforters, had breathless kisses in fresh air spiked with ocean and lavender. Our background music was the sound of waves rolling on shore and the lovely muffled clicking noise of the clothes dryer turning over.

I don't want sunbursts or marble halls.
I just want you. L.M. Montgomery ♥

The truth is that when one has gone to sleep in the midst of a fairy story and has wakened to find it real, one cannot be unhappy or keep the glow of joy out of one's eyes.
♥Frances Hodgson Burnett

Now I was the lady of the house, the girlfriend and support to the genius. I loved cooking for our friends, setting the table, making it pretty. More and more I made lunches and dinners for Cliff's business associates. I read cookbooks like novels, and Cliff gave me the keys to the castle: I could buy whatever I wanted at the kitchen shop downtown.

Because I didn't know any better, and because almost all the recipes I tried turned out well, I became fearless in the kitchen. I loved cooking for our friends. And if, for some strange reason, a recipe didn't work, I would just get a different one. And no recipe was too much trouble.

When I unmolded Julia's Charlotte Malakoff au Chocolat, with a whipped cream orange-almond-chocolate mousse filling ringed with tender homemade ladyfingers doused in Grand Marnier, the fans (as I like to call the people I love when I'm not calling them victims) went wild.

I fed them and they fed me, with their pleasure and their praise, which made me want to do more. I made patés, soufflés, and pastries for éclairs and croissants; crêpes, Pots de Crème au Chocolat, gravlax, Béarnaise, and Hollandaise; I stuffed, flambéed, roasted, and kneaded. Cliff was a very appreciative man who looked forward to coming home.

THE WAY TO A MAN'S HEART

Most of the time things turned out, but not always. I made a lemon ice that was so sweet it almost took the enamel off our teeth (not a Julia recipe). Two bites of it and I jumped up and ran around the table scooping bowls away from people saying, "No-no-no, you can't eat that!"

71

Cooking could also be the evening's entertainment. Once I made a cauliflower and potato soup that was too hot, then I filled the blender too full. When I turned it on, the lid blew off and the whole sloppy mess went all over the ceiling. The guests were in the kitchen like they always are ~ we stared, shocked, at the dripping ceiling, then at each other, then we exploded in laughter. I poured more wine and did not charge extra for the entertainment.

No one is born a great cook, one learns by doing. ♥ Julia Child

Once I burned up a stove because I didn't realize how important it was to clean the grease out of the broiler pan.

We were eating at the kitchen table with friends and just cutting into our steaks when I noticed tiny black specks swirling in front of my eyes.

Even though we were at least three blocks from the beach, I thought the specks were sand fleas or no-see-ums and tried to wave them away until we heard the crackling flames and saw smoke and realized the stove was on fire and those black things were falling ashes. Cliff jumped up and grabbed the fire extinguisher. I called the fire department, our guests took the food and drinks off the table and tried to help, not knowing if they should go or stay.

Trucks and sirens came roaring up our street to probably the most exciting dinner party we ever gave. Who doesn't love the chaos six big guys in fireman's clothes bring when they descend upon a nine-by-nine-foot kitchen with fire hoses? That's what I call a party!

My little sister Shelly came to stay with us for part of every summer ... she became my perfect little "Sue"-chef & apple-peeler extraordinaire.

After the fire was out and the kitchen was a sudsy mess, I passed around pieces of my rescued three-layer carrot cake to the firemen, lightly sprinkled with eau du stove ash.

Cliff had to buy a new stove, rebuild the cupboards next to it on both sides, and put in a partial new floor, but he wasn't mad at me, he took it very well. I think he was just grateful I didn't burn down the whole house.

I was not discouraged . . . I kept on cooking (paying closer attention to cleaning the broiler). As time went on I became more proficient and began to experiment with recipes.

Most of Julia's recipes, although no-fail and outrageously flavorful, complicated and delicious, required three or four days to make ~ some of them called for ingredients that were difficult, even impossible to find, either too modern or too French for our little out-back on the Central Coast. When I finally got everything home, washed,

Shelly at the company picnic at Lake Nacimiento in Paso Robles.

73

dried, julienned, deglazed, and sauced, my people devoured it all in 20 minutes. It seemed a lot to go through.

I liked recipes that tasted like they took three days to cook, but didn't. Some recipes, like my Baked Bananas, required only three ingredients, which I almost always had on hand. They took five minutes to make and were as good as any three-day dish I ever made. I honestly would have fed those bananas to Julia, and I'm sure she would have loved them (but not as much as I would have loved feeding them to her).

Baked Bananas with Ice Cream

Put one ripe, unpeeled banana (per person) on a cookie sheet. Bake at 350° until it turns completely black, about 20 min. Slit open & moosh up, same as you would with a baked potato. Serve w/ a scoop of vanilla ice cream & a sprinkle of fresh ground coffee. ♡

I wanted more recipes like that and started to experiment. I had a mantra for my idea of the perfect recipe: fast, easy, elegant, and delicious.

Methods, recipes, and ingredients have changed over the years. Food fads have come and gone, but Julia's the one who gave us our chops (in more ways than one). For me, all roads lead back to her. ♥

BEFORE JULIA CHILD THERE WAS ONLY ONION DIP.

You learn to cook so you don't have to be a slave to recipes. You get what's in season & you know what to do with it. ♡ *Julia Child*

*A*nd then he began to play so sweetly
that the poor girl stood as if
enchanted & her heart was
filled with joy. Grimm's Fairy Tales

Those who don't believe in magic
will never find it.

ROALD DAHL

Chapter Five
Back to the Future

Once in a while, right in the middle of an ordinary life, love gives us a fairy tale.
                                              Anon.

In the fall of 1976, Cliff took me to Boston for my first visit to New England. Boston wasn't our final destination ~ after a few days, we planned to meet up with Cliff's parents and drive to Cape Cod together and catch a ferry to a nearby island I'd never heard of called Martha's Vineyard. We were going to spend Thanksgiving in Vineyard Haven, where Cliff's grandmother, Lelia, and his two great aunts, Frances and Agatha, lived.

But before the arrival of Betty and Russ, we had four glorious days to enjoy Boston, a place I'd always wanted to see. On a chilly November morning, wearing a long purple wool coat I bor-rowed from one of Diana's nurse friends

What I did on the plane.

(California people rarely had long winter coats, but this girl came from Chicago), Cliff and I walked the Freedom Trail of Colonial Revolutionary Boston. It was the year of the Bicentennial. Our country was celebrating the 200th anniver-sary of the Declaration of Independence. For me, seeing the city for the first time ~ going to Old North Church, Paul Revere's House, the Old Corner Bookstore ~ and walking the narrow cobblestone streets, was like stepping into a history book and having it come alive.

Midnight Ride of Paul Revere, by A.L. Ripley

I'd been drawn to New England since I was a child. I always secretly felt like a part of me belonged there. My grandma was a member of the Daughters of the American Revolution, and when I was little, she showed me our family tree. One of our relatives graduated from Harvard College in 1756 and was the representative to the first U.S. Congress from New Hampshire. Another came from England on the Mayflower and kept a diary of the voyage. A third, I'm sorry to say ～ one of my great aunts, Elizabeth Howe ～ was hung in Salem in 1692 during the Witch Trials.

A PATRIOT, A WITCH & A DIARY-KEEPER...
MY KIND of PEOPLE. ♥

1628
THE *MAY FLOWER*
WILLIAM BRADFORD
1590~1657
@ ALICE (CARPENTER) SOUTHWORTH
1590-1670

A needlepoint gift my grandmother made for me, Christmas 1976.

Growing up, I loved books like *Little Women* and *Rebecca of Sunnybrook Farm*. In school I learned about Pilgrims, the Mayflower, and the Revolution. I had a crush on Walt Disney's Johnny Tremain and all the Sons of Liberty.

$\mathcal{I}$ connected to stories about George Washington and Abigail Adams, and especially I loved reading Benjamin Franklin's diary, which felt like a window to the past. I dreamed of charming New England houses with picket fences like I'd seen in old movies ~ filled with history and tradition.

FLAGS WERE EVERYWHERE!

$\mathcal{N}$ ow here I was, on a cold windy day in November, walking across Boston Common where my ancestors had walked, enjoying lovely old architecture where American flags flapped from every porch. We bought a flag for our house and sent several home for our friends as Christmas presents.

New England has a way of doing this to people; they can be homesick for it even if they have never seen it.
♥ Mark Van Doren

$\mathcal{W}$ e picked up Cliff's parents at the airport and drove south, through a gray drizzle, to Cape Cod. We stopped for an early dinner at a quaint little inn in Falmouth called The Nimrod (c. 1680), named for the British ship that opened fire on Falmouth during the War of 1812 and shot a cannonball through the building. The hole was still there.

Paul Revere's house! Oldest in downtown Boston, built in 1680.

It was dark and cozy and OLD inside, with a rough-hewn beamed ceiling, wood paneling and floor, and fireplaces (with no screens) blazing in every room. I was no longer stepping back in time. I had moved in.

I had an old-fashioned dessert I'd never heard of: a local specialty called Indian pudding. It was served hot with vanilla ice cream and was dark with cinnamon, ginger, brown sugar, molasses and plump raisins. Mmmmmmm. I made a list of what I thought was in it, hoping I could re-create it when we got back home. (Which I did, and here's what I came up with. I've made it lots of times, it's tried and true:)

Indian Pudding

5½ c. whole milk
2/3 c. cornmeal
4 Tbsp. butter
½ c. maple syrup
¼ c. molasses

1 tsp. ginger
1 tsp. cinnamon
½ tsp. salt
1 c. raisins
vanilla ice cream

300° Serves 8

Preheat oven to 300°. Butter a small casserole ~ mine is 6½" x 10½". Over med. heat, in a large saucepan, scald the milk but don't boil it. Slowly whisk in cornmeal & continue to stir until mixture begins to thicken ~ 10 min. or so. Add remaining ingredients & keep stirring till heated through. Pour into casserole & bake 3 hours till sides are brown & sticky-looking. (The pudding hardens a bit as it cools.) Serve warm with vanilla ice cream. ♥

80

From there we drove down to Woods Hole and boarded a ferry to Vineyard Haven. The boat looked like a big white shoebox with windows and a smokestack. The whistle blew, the ferry churned the water into white froth, and we slowly pulled away from the dock.

We plowed through the waves past a lonely-looking lighthouse on the shore of the 100-square-mile island seven miles off the coast of Massachusetts. I had a little guidebook that said that Martha's Vineyard was named in 1602 by the explorer Bartholomew Gosnold, for his daughter Martha and for the wild grapevines that grew there. I learned that it was already a thriving Native American community when my diary-keeping ancestor arrived in Plymouth in 1620 ~ and that now it was a popular vacation spot for celebrities, writers and actors, and regular families, too. The year-round population comprised fishermen, carpenters, plumbers, merchants, doctors, lawyers, teachers, and nurses.

CAPE COD FOLKS

Cliff's grandmother's gray-shingled cottage was built in 1872 on the shore of a large lagoon. The ceilings were low, the fireplace was huge, the floors were wide wood boards, worn and burnished with age that shone in the firelight. The glass panes in our bedroom windows were bubbly and rippled, making the view across the garden down to the pond look like an Impressionist watercolor.

81

It was quiet. All we heard was the floor creaking, the hissing of the fire, wind and rain tapping the windows ~ cup connecting with saucer, newspaper pages turning. While Lelia and Betty visited and drank tea in front of the fire, Cliff and Russ read the paper, and I made bread and butter pudding in Lelia's kitchen. Sugar, cream, butter, and egg yolks made the little house smell wonderful on a cold rainy day.

We were only on the Island for three days. It was dark and drizzly most of the time, but that did not dampen the visit for me. In fact, it made it better. California did not have crisp raw winds, wild cries of gulls, and log fires burning everywhere we went.

MAIN STREET, VINEYARD HAVEN

Photo taken in the 1930s but Vineyard Haven still looked the same.

82

Lelia's

Cliff and I drove down the short Main Street bordered on both sides by two-story, 19th-century wooden buildings painted white, with gables, second-floor porches, leaded windows, and decorative trim. Commercial businesses, shops, and drugstores were housed in these homey-looking structures. There were large trees ∼ most of the leaves were gone, but the branches sheltered the street and made the town really look like a "Haven."

Cliff said, looking out the car windows, "Wow, this place is OLD." I heard a little veto in his voice. "Old everything ∼ old cars, old houses, old people . . ." (He woke up in a bad mood, he wasn't wild about the narrow twin beds in his grandmother's guest room, the tight blankets crushed his teeny-tiny toes.)

Besides his parents and 90-year-old grandmother, we had Thanksgiving dinner with his two great aunts, one of whom had a boyfriend named Nelson. They were all sharp and chatty, in their late 80s and early 90s, and all dressed up for the holiday.

Cliff went on, "I haven't seen a car newer than around 1958. What do you think they do for fun around here? I don't know how anyone could live out in the middle of nowhere on this midget island. How do they get their mail? Tugboat? Maybe if I was 103. Oh my God, did you see the newspaper? What was it? Four pages of Billy saw a blackbird? Probably nothing ever happens here, that's all they have to write about. It's already getting dark. What is it? Three p.m.? And those windows at Lelia's, they're so small you can't see out of them. It's freezing and it's going to stay that way for the next six months. How do they stand it? I was freezing last night, weren't you? You probably have to pay a fortune just for sweaters and coats; look at these people, they are completely buttoned up. Look at the little guy trying to cross the street, he can't even see out from under that hat. How much do you think they pay for heat? They probably have to chop wood all winter just to stay alive." A stream of unconsciousness.

I was in tears laughing at his tirade ～ I was already in love with the place. But I could just picture how ridiculous Cliff's car would look on these narrow old roads where the speed limit was 25 miles an hour. I didn't think we would blend.

As we drove out of town, we passed dry stone walls and picket fences, and sprawling summer houses, generations old, with wide porches fronted by columns and lattice, hedges and long, leaf-strewn lawns overlooking the white-capped water. Everything looked closed-up; there weren't many signs of life.

"Oh, Cliff! Slow down! Look at that little graveyard! I wonder if we can go in? The gate's open! Stop the car!"

84

He pulled over, the tires crunching gravel. I sat there looking at a lovely neighborhood cemetery.

"Talk about old," I said out loud. "I have to go see this. Do you want to come? Or can you wait while I go in? Just for a minute? It's not very big."

"You want to walk around a graveyard in the rain? Isn't that a little weird? No," he said, shaking his head, "I don't think so. You go. It's cold out there. I'll wait. But hurry. Scream if you see a frozen ghost and I'll come save you."

TIMELESS

I laughed and opened my umbrella as I got out of the car. I pushed on the low white gate and the rusty hinges creaked as I stepped inside. It was not one bit weird, not a frozen ghost in sight. It was beautiful and old and real and familiar, I felt like I'd been there before.

The feeling got stronger as I stood among the stones listening to the raindrops patter my umbrella ~ in the yellow grass with the smell of rain and moldering leaves, my scarf blowing in the wind, reading mysterious names carved into headstones etched in green moss under dripping trees that seemed to be whispering ancient prayers.

THE ONLY FEELING STRONGER THAN LOSS IS LOVE. ♥

Watching my step on the uneven ground, I wandered from stone to stone reading inscriptions. There were grave markers in all sizes and shapes, some carved with cherub faces, some with angels wings, and some with skulls. The oldest one was dated 1791. Some were cracked and beginning to crumble; on some the names were gone, worn off by centuries of weather and salt air.

Under wet slate and stone, with leaves skittering across the grass and gathering against the markers, adored wives, honored husbands, beloved children, generations of people who'd lived their lives on this island so many years ago, slept. It seemed to be much more about life than death, something enduring and historic. It was like I pulled back a watery curtain between the past and present. I could picture those lives. I felt a connection. Passing time came up from the earth and anchored me there.

I have been here before,
But how or when I cannot tell;
I know the grass beyond the door,
The sweet keen smell,
The sighing sound,
The lights around the shore.
♥ Dante Gabriel Rossetti

with sixty diamond minutes.

Chapter Six
Jupiter Aligns with Mars

And the herdsman had seen in the girl's eyes a world just like that: a world of wonder, a world not of grass & wild creatures but of human glances. A world of things that dwell in the heart. ♥ FRENCH FAIRY TALES

Back in California there was a carefree everydayness to our lives. Cliff was working like crazy, but he made sure to get home in time for dinner. I loved making a home and was happy in my world. Our house rocked with music all the time: the Beatles, Eric Clapton, Al Green, Dan Hicks, Linda Ronstadt, the Eagles, Rod Stewart, Gordon Lightfoot, James Taylor, Fleetwood Mac, and the Doobie Brothers.

Cliff laughed and rolled his eyes when I slipped in my Marilyn Monroe and Shirley Temple albums. He didn't really understand my love for Frank Sinatra's music ("You see a pair of laughing eyes, and suddenly you're sighing sighs . . ." How could he not?), which is why I didn't play it while he was around. As far as he was concerned, Jimmy Durante and Marilyn Monroe had no business singing at all, ever. He didn't get the point of Edith Piaf, either, since she didn't sing in English ~ and forget about Fred Astaire ~ the dancing guy who wore a scarf around his waist instead of a belt? Please.

I liked Cliff's parents' music just as much as ours; and sometimes, for instance, as background music for a dinner party, I liked it better. I thought it was romantic when candles were lit and dinner was served, as though we were living in one of the old movies I loved to watch on TV. When Cliff wasn't around I put on Fred Astaire and sang "A Fine Romance" and danced from stove to sink to fridge while making dinner.

Sometimes Cliff and I would meet in town to go to the movies or dinner, each in our own car, and race each other home on the old road that ran next to the freeway, me chasing behind him trying to keep up but not as brave as he was. We weaved in and out, speeding up, slowing down, singing to the music, laughing out loud, young, crazy, and madly in love.

Cliff didn't want me to work. He liked me to be home, to make dinner, entertain our friends, to be with him when he traveled, and make sure his T-shirts were organized (I folded them so the logos were on the outside, and filed them on edge across his drawers so that he could see them all at the same time ~ he was very impressed). My job was to make sure he was never out of toothpaste or shampoo or Snickers bars, and that was fine with me, too ~ in fact, put a little check mark in the box that said, "Susie's dream come true." ✓

When Cliff answered the phone, instead of "Hello," he said, "Paradise." It thrilled my heart to hear him do that. I felt proud. My guy thought his home was paradise. What more could a girl ask for?

had plenty to do taking care of the house and our social calendar, but I did wish I had some sort of little job. I had this idea to make and sell decorative pillows. I made a whole bunch of them, ruffled, embroidered, buttoned and pieced, and a girlfriend let me put them in her gift store in the Network (on consignment), next door to Stereo West. Here are some of them:

Unfortunately, they didn't sell, not even one (what is wrong with people) ～ which meant I would not be going into the pillow business after all. It wasn't a complete failure, because now my sisters and I would have pillows to last a lifetime. ♡

esides sewing pillows, I baked cakes and casseroles, embroidered apples on napkins, made curtains, arranged flowers, appliquéd dish towels, cross-stitched wall hangings, and made Christmas gifts. I was decorating and creating a real home for the first time, and I couldn't get enough of it.

If you asked him, Cliff would have said that he wasn't a romantic guy, but I knew differently. He had a deep and abiding understanding of girls and their feelings about jewelry, which resulted in surprise gifts that would make anyone feel loved. In fact he understood it before I did. He was my jewelry teacher. We went to see the movie *The Sailor Who Fell from Grace with the Sea*, and the female lead wore beautiful pearls in almost every scene. The next day Cliff handed me a box festooned with ribbons and filled with a string of pearls. Elizabeth Montgomery wore a diamond heart on a chain around her neck in the TV show, *Bewitched*, and for Christmas, there was a diamond heart just like hers, for me. One birthday there was a brand new gold VW, tied up with a giant pink ribbon, waiting in the driveway.

Sometimes Cliff brought his business partners home and I made lunch for them. Other days, I made his lunch and took it to the office. I needed kisses in the middle of the day, and he was the one who had them.

BLISSED OUT

Cliff's business was growing fast. He and Tom had renovated a three-story brick warehouse over by the train station and moved the offices and the mail-order division out of the store basement into the new building. They separated the mail-order division from Stereo West and called it Warehouse Sound Company. They also opened four new stores along the Central Coast. Cliff was consumed with the details and excited about the future.

Here's a photo of the Warehouse before renovation, with all of us dressed like characters from the 1920s to match the new building ~ Bonnie and Clyde sell music systems.

ME CLIFF TOM ELAINE

At 5 a.m., Cliff would wake up with a brainstorm and his feet would begin to twitch. Pretty soon he'd leap out of bed and run to the typewriter. I'd get up and make him Ovaltine and Cream of Rice, sneak up behind him, kiss his neck. He would barely know I was there, he was so lost in his thoughts. An hour later he'd be flying down the driveway in his car, running off to manifest his dream before the next one grabbed his attention.

Dark Clouds

Something in the Water

Every time we say goodbye, I die a little...

Despite how lucky and happy we were (from my perspective at least), domestic bliss was not a constant thing. We broke up at least once a year for the first four years we were together. We'd be going along fine and then suddenly Cliff would become restless and distant and I would know he wanted out. He was young, handsome and successful. Girls threw themselves at him everywhere he went, but not quite as enthusiastically, it seemed to me, as he threw himself at them.

You can just imagine how much it killed me each time I realized someone new had caught his eye. It proved his point: life wasn't always roses. He would never say, "Let's break up," or ask me to move out; he would just be miserable and uninterested until I couldn't take it anymore. Burying my head in the sand, pleading for communication, demanding explanations, and going around half-crazed got old after a while.

Sooner or later I'd see the situation for what it was, and what it was, was usually blond. I'd be forced to muster up at least a decent imitation of self-respect, pack my clothes and my Beatrix Potter people and go.

It was always very public, and I was always devastated. I wished I had some sort of mask to wear, something to hide behind. With my confidence at a new low, I'd move in with a girlfriend, get a job, and try to start over. Once a year for four years, some version of this would happen, and I was always the one to go. After all, it was his house.

Then the blue shadows will fall all over town...
Ronnie Milsap

During these separations, I stayed as far away from him as possible. I did not drop by, I did not drive by, I did not call. If he wanted me, he knew where I was. I would not give him the privilege of seeing me miserable or even seeing me at all. Of course ~ big fish, little pond ~ our breakups were fodder for the gossip mill in our little town and hard to escape. Everyone wanted to talk to me about him, asking me how I felt, and what was going to happen. How did I know what was going to happen? I wasn't in charge. I would put on a fake brave face, cry buckets with my girlfriends, get a job as a waitress, go on fake dates and out fake dancing while he romped around SLO with his new girlfriend in his Lamborghini or whatever zippity-doo-dah car du jour he had at the time.

93

Each time it happened I'd be more aware that by being with Cliff, I was digging myself into a hole. I had chosen to ignore the fact that he wasn't anxious to get married and felt the same way about having children as he did about coffee tables. I always thought, home and family, wasn't that what everyone wanted? Wasn't that just what people DO? No, surprisingly, not everyone. Some people prefer to slither around town with blond strangers. As my mom would say, "It takes all kinds."

I'VE GOT YOU

♪...Use your mentality, wake up to reality...♫

UNDER MY SKIN

While we were broken up, I would get a good look at the independent, self-reliant-woman thing, all the rage in the early '70s, at least on paper. The problem was, I'd never planned a life of my own. I had no idea how it was done. Also, independence didn't include Cliff, and I was crazy about him ∼ "crazy" being the operative word.

After a month or two, he would get bored with his new girl. Sooner or later, he would come find me. I'd open the door of my apartment, and there he would be, all cute and sheepish. He'd tell me how sorry he was, what a mistake he'd made, what a moron the girl turned out to be (somehow he meant this to be a compliment, but if you look, you can see that she and I actually had a lot in common). He would remind me I was three years ahead of him, more mature, and tell me how stupid he'd been. Yes, yes, I would agree with him, standing back with arms folded like steel.

TALK TO THE HAND

94

Grateful for my "understanding" and "patience," he'd pull me to him, wipe my tears, uncurl my claws, pet my hair, kiss me until my knees were weak and he would smell so good that I would lose my resolve, get giddy with happiness, and move back in with him. We'd be in mad love and happy for months ~ until the next time.

If you cry, catch your tears in a cup, sprinkle them on your lover's pillow ~ he will experience a great change of heart.

It became an almost-predictable pattern: rescue, promise, cheat, and destroy, leading right back to rescue, promise, cheat, and destroy. It's perfectly clear now, but at the time, because it came in waves, I never thought it would happen again. Each time I tried not to take him back. I really did. But I think you can see that whatever Lola wanted, Lola got, and I could not refuse. I was melted Jell-O when he came around. No edges at all. Mush.

I spent my entire 20s like this. When we were happy (which we were 85% of the time), it was "paradise" ~ but when we weren't, it was hell on wheels.

A lot of my girlfriends were going through this same thing. It seemed to be a 1970s epidemic. We thought there might be something in the water, there was so much trial and error. Every woman handled it differently. Some left the guy and suffered in silence; some stayed and lost a piece of their soul. It was awful no matter what you decided to do.

fter the second time we broke up, I began to see this thing as a pattern. The third time I left Cliff, I went farther away. In case he tried to come get me, it wouldn't be so easy. I moved two and a half hours north to Carmel, rented an apartment and got a job and was there for four months without my friends or the touchstones of my former life, trying to forget him, find a foothold, and start over. And then one day he showed up at my door and sweet-talked me into coming home with him using his best sales pitch (the one he used when he sold air conditioners to Eskimos), hitching up his cute corduroy pants, batting his Jeff Bridges eyes at me.

TROUBLE IN RIVER CITY

s usual, I didn't make it difficult for him ～ I could go, but I could never stay gone. I was a pushover when he professed his true love and promised me the moon and said, "Don't you know we belong together?" with the cutest smile and most darling ruffled hair. He kissed me passionately in the soft leather seats of his ridiculously fast car, turned up the music, rolled down the windows, and we sang all the way home,

"'Cause you're fine & you're mine & you look so divine..."
♥ REDBONE

ME.

All I know is that I was never away long enough to get over him and start fresh. I was the block of wood at the end of the yo-yo string: throw it out, bring it back. I don't remember consciously choosing this route. It was more like my footprints were already there and I had to step into them and follow wherever they were going.

— • — • THE NORMAL ONE — • — • —

We did fine as long as we lived within the confines of the traditions we grew up with: me as subservient homemaker, him as monogamous breadwinner. Any break from that meant a clash of the Titans. But, of course, we couldn't see it at all. And deep inside, I wasn't subservient. And he wasn't monogamous.

Nothing ever happens by accident. I must have needed to climb into a hole in order to be inspired in the climbing-out-of-it phase to never let it happen again, and to get on with whatever it was I needed to get on with. But before my life got completely ruined, one more nail needed to be pounded into the coffin.

I needed to marry him.

*Say nighty-night & kiss me,
just hold me tight & tell me you miss me,
when I'm alone & blue as can be,
dream a little dream of me...*
♥ Mama Cass

When they came
to the little
house they saw
that it was built
of bread & covered
with cakes with
windows of
clear sugar.

Hansel & Gretel

1976

The fifth year of our relationship, when Cliff was 26 and I was 29, things between us were better than they'd ever been; it really felt like we'd turned a corner. Cliff had started building a wonderful house on 10 acres in a little valley just outside of town at the foot of an oak-covered hill ~ a house that had as much me in it as him.

Diana's boyfriend, Paul, was the architect. We spent lots of time on the lot while Paul drew up the plans ~ I'd sit on the ground and read while Cliff paced over the property figuring out orientations. At night we studied the plans, adding windows, measuring the kitchen table to make sure it would fit, figuring out where the electrical outlets would go. As the house was being framed, we walked the floor plan again and again, considering every detail, loving the smell of new-cut wood, thinking how nice it was going to be to sleep with the sound of the train whistle from the valley below.

Before we started building

The new driveway (ie racetrack)

99

ogether we chose sinks, faucets, paint colors, doorknobs, tile, wallpaper, carpet. I liked double-hung "criss-cross" windows like the ones in Cliff's grandmother's house and Cliff wanted modern windows of mitered plate glass, so we planned for both. I liked the idea

of a brick or rock fireplace; he wanted tile so he kindly gave me the choice of which tile. I chose three-by-eight-inch green tiles ∼ because I thought they would look good at Christmas ∼ and because I was an idiot.

Paul, with his wild Einstein hair and leprechaun-blue eyes, thought we did very well considering our style differences: Cliff's modern sensibility vs. "the doily mentality" (that's what these guys called my decorating style). Paul was worried because he'd "built a lot of divorces" in his time.

For us, it was just the opposite. While our house was going up, Cliff and I went away for a long weekend to the lovely PINK La Valencia Hotel in La Jolla. While swimming in the hotel pool overlooking palm trees and the Pacific Ocean, Cliff asked, "Will you marry me?" I splashed into his arms saying, "Yes! yes! yes!" (Actually to be honest, what he said

was more like, "OK, I'll marry you." But it was still totally unexpected. Happy tears popped from my eyes, exactly as if he'd thought of it all by himself.)

alking around through town under the stars that balmy evening, we went into a jewelry store where he bought me an eternity band with tiny sparkly diamonds that went all the way around my finger. There are no words for my joy that day. We were getting married! We would say we loved each other in front of everyone! We would have a garden and I would cook and we would live happily ever after ~ for eternity, to match my new ring.

e set the date for eight months later. We decided to have the ceremony on the hill under the oaks in the backyard of our new house a month after it was supposed to be finished ~ on Saturday, June 25, 1977.

hen we told Cliff's mom, she threw her arms around me and we stood in that embrace, cheek to cheek, looking at Cliff with sparkling, watery eyes, both of us in awe of his genius for having this wonderful idea to finally marry me. His dad cut in and gave me a big hug and said, "Welcome to the family!" My whole family was thrilled, too ~ especially my youngest sister, Shelly, who was 16 by then but had dreamed of being my flower girl since she was 10 and wasn't about to give up on it now. She immediately began to plan her outfit.

After six years together, none of our friends were surprised to hear we were getting married. Everyone was happy for us and up for a party, especially a wedding: the perfect way to christen our new house. Cliff's best friend, Jim, warned me, laughing, "You're marrying *him*? You'll be sorry!" I started singing "Sadie, Sadie, Married Lady" around the house. Cliff, of course, loved that.

"*I* do my nails, read up on sales,
all day the records play..."

♥ ♥ ♥ ♥ ♥ ♥

In March 1977, while the wood floor was being laid in our new kitchen, Cliff took me on my first trip ever to Europe for what we called our "pre-honeymoon." He'd been invited to give a speech at the Consumer Electronics Show being held in Madrid, Spain, which was the real reason for the trip. All the big wheels from Sony, JBL, Harman Kardon, Bose, and Pioneer would be there.

Cliff's youth, and his success in marketing their products to young people, were attracting lots of attention, making him kind of a spokesperson for the Pepsi Generation. They all wanted to hear what the whiz kid had to say. He wanted me to go with him and said we would take a side trip to London before we went on to Madrid. I weighed the pros and cons as to whether or not I should go. Con: Eleven hours in flying coffin? Or Pro: London and Madrid. London and Madrid! Are you kidding? I was so excited!

e landed safely at Heathrow Airport and climbed into a boxy black taxicab that took us (notably and alarmingly and clearly unsafely, on the wrong side of the road) to the Grosvenor House Hotel facing Hyde Park. The hotel was built in the 1920s and had a cavernous two-story lobby that looked like a wedding cake frosted in marble and gold with a gallery dripping in carved garlands. Masses of white roses in clear-cut vases decorated the public rooms. There were crystal chandeliers, huge arched doorways framed by columns, a grand staircase, marble floors, and Oriental carpets the size of football fields.

e were jet-lagged the first day, so we took it easy ∼ eating, napping, and walking along the Thames, but not much else. I woke up our second morning feeling rested, humming (because I couldn't help myself), "En-ga-land swings like a pendulum do," happy to be on the ground and not in an airplane, looking out the windows at the foggy street filled with old buildings,

listening to Big Ben chime. Room service brought us breakfast: tea and crumpets and jam on a damask-draped silver tray with smooth linen napkins the size of pillowcases. I was excited to go out. I was hoping we could walk over and see the changing of the guard at Buckingham Palace.

I was dressed and ready to go, but Cliff hadn't moved from the bed.

"You go," he said, burrowing down farther between the pillows and under the covers. "I need to work on my speech. There's a map there on the dresser. It's only a few blocks over; it's a palace, you can't miss it."

"You're not coming?" WAH

"No, go ahead and go. I'll work on the speech ~ I'll be ready when you get back. Here, give me the map and I'll show you."

So that's what I did. I took my map and window-shopped in the general direction of the palace, down a charming cobbled street filled with boutiques, kitchen shops, shoe stores, and flower shops in buildings straight out of Dickens.

It began to rain just as I was walking by a little brick shop called Paris. Behind a milky blue window box overflowing with forget-me-nots and pink phlox, on the other side of the rain-spattered window, was the prettiest umbrella, open and covered in small yellow and lilac flowers. I hurried through the wooden shop door with its tinkling bell to buy this precious thing. The rain was perfectly timed to give me the quintessential London souvenir. And something more.

Paris of London

Inside the shop my eyes fell on an antique dress form wearing the most wonderful four-piece dress. In fact, the moment I saw it, I knew I'd found, without even looking, my perfect wedding dress. It was right out of an American girl's dream of what a Carnaby Street, Victorian, "wear-your-love-like-heaven" fashion statement should be.

It wasn't fancy, it wasn't satin, it didn't go to the floor or have 300 covered buttons going up the back or "yards of skirt" (as Audrey Hepburn in Sabrina would say). There was no "designer" name on it, but it was perfect for me: cutwork white-cotton lace and little ribbons. There was a camisole with lace straps, tied with ribbons at the waist, which could be worn with or without a matching cap-sleeved jacket. If you wore the camisole alone, there was a separate eyelet piece about an inch wide to tie around your neck. The skirt fell just below the knee with an eyelet-ruffled hem and lace panels.

Looking at it, touching it, wanting it, I forgot all about the changing of the guard and only thought about the changing of the clothes. I went to the fitting room and tried it on; I twirled and pranced in the three-way mirror. I put the jacket on, I tied on the neck piece, I took off the jacket. I did all of this three times. The English salesgirls came back to look. They loved it and said it was "smashin'" and "brilliant." So I bought it.

I got back to the hotel room with my darling umbrella and my smashing dress in a big tissue-filled box with joy-of-moment written all over my face. Cliff was still sprawled in the middle of the bed, his back propped against a pile of pillows, surrounded with papers. Rain was dribbling down the long panes of glass, the silvery drops racing to catch up with one another.

"WAIT 'TIL I SHOW YOU!" I said, digging into the box and tossing tissue into the air. Possibly unwise, due to the old superstition about the groom seeing the dress before the wedding ～ bad luck and all that rot. But I couldn't help it. I told myself that rule didn't count when you were in another country.

He loved the dress. I stood on my toes and spun around, put on the jacket and tied all the little bows, took it off again and twirled around the room. He watched indulgently, shook his head with a little smile and said sweetly, "Come here, fairy tale girl, and let me see how those little ribbon things work."

They slipped briskly into an intimacy from which they never recovered. ♥ F. Scott Fitzgerald

Later, immersed in bubbles and hot water in the deep porcelain tub in the shiny white-tiled bathroom, holding up my book to keep it dry, I called to Cliff, "It's almost four o'clock. Can we go down for tea?"

I drank tea every morning . . . but this was different ～ a real, English "Afternoon Tea" ～ I'd read about it but this would be my first.

Cliff liked dirt bikes, fast cars, and rock and roll; he wasn't really crazy about the idea of formal "tea." His big-man fingers were wide and flat like my dad's old leather catcher's mitt ～ he had trouble holding on to those fragile flowery little teacups.

But he went for me ~ and he did like the chocolate éclairs and napoleons very much. He thought the soft little crustless tea sandwiches were almost like Fritos, the way they popped into your mouth, and you could never eat just one.

There were bluebells on every table, rain poured down the windows, cups clinked softly into their saucers, and a piano played "La Vie en Rose," which just happened to be my favorite song ever. It was all I hoped it would be, total nirvana for the doily mentality. 💜

A little thing like tea... magic!

Nothing can be truer than fairy wisdom. It's as true as Sunbeams. 💜 Douglas Jerrold

They were so madly
in love with the
little house
that they could not bear
to think they
had finished it.

J. M. Barrie

CHAPTER SEVEN

Before she knew 'twas art...

♥ *L.M. Alcott*

We got home from England at the end of March 1977 and moved everything into our new house ~ although there were lots of missing light fixtures, closet doors and knobs, things like that. I swept out the sawdust, made the beds, fluffed pillows, arranged books on shelves, put soap and shampoo in the shower, tacked shelf paper in the kitchen, organized cupboards and drawers and filled them with dishes and silverware, put food in the fridge, hung pots and pans over my new kitchen island, and loved every moment of it. And I started to make preparations for our wedding in June.

We were at Cliff's parents' for dinner. I was telling his mom and dad about our trip to England and Madrid and what a star Cliff had been giving his speech, how funny he was and how the audience had laughed and clapped and given him a standing ovation. Cliff, only 26, a kid really, had the whole room of 50-year-old executives in the palm of his hand. His cockiness made them laugh; his youth energized them. He wasn't a bit nervous. He posed his own questions with funny answers; he kept everyone on their toes.

told Russ and Betty I'd stood in the back of the room leaning against the wall, watching him race back and forth on stage (wearing a T-shirt and hitching up his cords), listening, with my hands clasped to my chest, so proud, thinking, *Wow, is he just the bravest person in the world or what?*

I glanced from his mom over to Cliff ~ he was beaming. His mom looked at him, then back at me. She said, "Susie, you should see your face. The way you look at him!"

liff knew he was good, and he was. He was great! His dad leaned over to him, put his hand on his shoulder, and said, "Good job, Son." It was a very sweet moment.

"WHO LOOKS AT YOU THE WAY I DO?...WHEN YOU SMILE, I CAN TELL, WE KNOW EACH OTHER VERY WELL..."
♥ Dionne Warwick

So far 30 is much better than 20!

A P R I L 1 9 7 7

or my 30th birthday we had our first dinner party in the new house for 10 of our favorite people. I baked a chocolate cake and made lemon chicken, Parmesan linguini, roasted carrots, and spinach salad with bacon and home-made croutons. We had the first fire in our new (green) fireplace and Frank sang "She gets too hungry for dinner at eight . . ." It was perfect. Cliff surprised me with a beautiful gold watch with a circle of diamonds around the face. It was a wonderful evening, but what turned out to be the best present of all came from Diana ~ a gift certificate to Graham's art store. She knew I liked to make things and thought I might find something good there. 💜

MAKE A WISH

Graham's was downtown on Monterey Street. It wasn't an arts and crafts store ~ otherwise, I would have used the gift certificate for fabric or yarn. Graham's was a fine art store where they sold oil paints, easels, and canvas. I had no idea what I might buy there. I was not an artist. The only time I'd held a paintbrush (except for when I painted my bedroom, which probably didn't count) was in kindergarten.

I wandered around, looking at what they had, moving the arms on the wooden mannequins, admiring the thick French watercolor paper and the array of richly colored chalk pastels. I gazed at all the differently shaped brushes, the calligraphy pens, jars of colored ink, tubes and boxes of watercolors. It was a little overwhelming ~ I didn't know what most of it was and definitely had no idea what to do with it.

111

A man wearing a leather apron approached, introduced himself as Dan, and asked if he could help.

I showed him my gift certificate and told him I wasn't sure, but I was thinking about getting some watercolors. I held up a paint box and asked, "Are paint boxes good? Or are the tubes of paint better?"

I thought I might try watercolors because at least I knew from kindergarten that all you had to do was mix the paint with water. I figured I could handle that.

"It depends on what you want to do."

I told him I didn't know what I wanted to do. I'd never done it before.

He gave me advice on the different products and explained my choices to me. I bought a large pad of heavy textured French paper called D'Arches, three sizes of brushes, a Pelikan paintbox, and a metal ruler. He said if I wanted to sketch first, I would need pencils, a soft eraser, and a small plastic pencil sharpener, so I got them, too.

As I was leaving the shop he called out to me, "Don't forget to bring me your masterpieces. I do framing, too!"

"Sure," I laughed back at him, "you can count on the masterpieces!"

I read somewhere that "inspiration" derives from the Latin words sanctus espiritus, which means the breath of God. Breath of God: A lovely thought all by itself ~ it makes perfect sense to have Providence whispering; otherwise, there's too much left unexplained.

Providence wakes each morning
an hour before the sun.
French Folktales

DEEPLY HIDDEN TALENT

I'm sure the very first "drawing" I did was when I was four and learned to write my name. To a child, making letters curve just right for the first time, getting little fingers with lives of their own to do the bidding of the mind and make a J or an S, is as difficult, and almost the same, as trying to draw a flower.

My only real "art lesson" came in the seventh grade when we were given a choice between two classes: art or music. I chose art. We never touched a paintbrush in that class. Instead,

I've always thought my kindergarten art explained something profound about the two sides of my brain, but I was never sure what. Love the clouds though.

the teacher had us draw our own thumbs on newsprint in pencil almost all semester long. She was smart and used what she had; her students came equipped with their own built-in life-drawing models.

"See the groove around the sides of your thumbnail?" My teacher held up her thumb to demonstrate. "See how your thumb is wider at the top; see how it curves inward before it widens out to meet the rest of your hand? You can measure that distance with your eyes. Ask yourself: The narrowest part of the thumb is where in relation to the bottom of your thumbnail? See how it's a bit darker on the sides than it is in the middle?"

She taught us to really *look* at our subject, to see the light and dark, the equal and unequal aspects of each side; and she taught us how we could shade our drawings by smudging the pencil lines. What a good teacher she was. With only a pencil, she taught all that.

I got an A in that class, but since it was an elective, I thought everyone got an A. My thumb drawings offered no sudden revelation, and nothing made me think I should take more art classes; no adult made mention of it, as far as I knew. And it's not that I wasn't interested; I just didn't think I was any better at it than anyone else. In fact, probably at the time, I didn't think anyone did ANYTHING better than someone else, except maybe Annette Funicello. I thought the rest of us were all alike. I was only 12. It was just one more thing they told us to do that I could check off my list that would be an easy A that made my parents happy. The rest of the time I drew stick figures and played Hangman and scribbled hearts and flowers all over my notebooks just like everyone else.

A child her wayward pencil drew
On margins of her book.;
Garlands of flowers, dancing elves,
Bud, butterfly and brook,
Lessons undone, and plumb forgot,
Seeking with hand & heart
The teacher whom she learned to love
Before she knew, 'twas art.

Louisa May Alcott

Then one rainy afternoon when I was 18, I was sitting alone in my apartment about to write a letter to my grandma, listening to music. There was a Barbra Streisand album sitting on the couch next to me with a black-and-white close-up photograph of her face on the cover. I'd been writing on a pad of lined paper, but I started fooling around with the pencil, copying Barbra's face from the album onto the paper.

ust like I was taught in the seventh grade, I looked to see the distance between the corners of her eyes, where her nostril was in relation to the pupil of her eye, the distance between the bottom of her nose to her lip. I rubbed the pencil marks to shade her Cleopatra eyeliner, her hair and the shadows on the sides of her face until my thumb was smudged with graphite. Wow, I thought to myself when it was done, this is kind of a surprise ~ it looks like Barbra Streisand. But that was all. I didn't show it to anyone. I threw it away.

couple of years later, I did the same thing with an old black-and-white photo of my grandma. That's when it occurred to me that maybe I could draw.

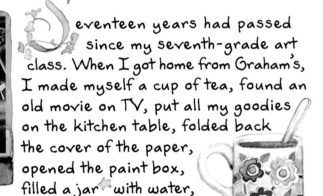

eventeen years had passed since my seventh-grade art class. When I got home from Graham's, I made myself a cup of tea, found an old movie on TV, put all my goodies on the kitchen table, folded back the cover of the paper, opened the paint box, filled a jar with water, sharpened my pencil, and looked around for something to draw.

here was a geranium in a clay pot on the table that looked like a good candidate. I pushed it out in front of me and turned it the way you would turn a Christmas tree, trying to find the best side. I gave it a critical look and thought, Okay, how do you do this? Where do you start?

ince then I've asked myself that question a thousand times.

I discovered, in what has always felt like "the hard way," that when doing something I've never done before I had to make stuff up, find a way, invent. If you're intent on making a path through the woods and you come to a tree that's in the way, the tree has to go or the path has to change course. You keep making those choices until you have your path. After the thing was done, I realized, You just do it ∿ that's how you do it. You have to figure it out.

"THERE AIN'T NO RULES AROUND HERE," said Thomas Edison, "WE'RE TRYING TO ACCOMPLISH SOMETHING."

So, first I drew the pot, looking at my model, then back at the paper, trying to make both sides of the pot as equal as I could, erasing, drawing, erasing, and trying again. I sketched the stems of the geranium, noting their different widths, then the leaves, looking from paper to plant, gauging the distance between them, measuring with my eyes the size of one leaf and comparing it to the one next to it. When I couldn't see what else I should add, I stopped and fixed another cup of tea, because now I was at the scary part ∿ I had to put on the paint ∿ an eraser couldn't help me anymore. I decided to make the paper a little wet first, I swirled my brush in the water and filled in the drawing of the clay pot with plain water.

⭐ I bought this little jar at Disneyland (as a souvenir) about two weeks before I did my first painting. I've used it for water for painting ever since.

117

In the very first of a long lifetime of moments of truth (each of them just as scary as the one before), I mixed brown paint with orange to try to match the color of the pot. I swished the brush round and round in the paint, adding more water and more paint until it was good and thick. I touched the brush to the wet spot on the paper; it burst and spread like fireworks. While the paint was still very damp I added dark brown to blend and shadow the sides and make the pot look rounded. I kept looking from my subject to my watercolor and back, doing my best to copy it, looking for the lightest parts and the darkest, filling in watered leaves with green paint, using darker green in some places, leaving thin lines for veins in the leaves, and saving the small, unopened, pinkish-red geranium buds for last.

And then it was finished and that was it. I thought I might sign my name because, to me, shockingly, it actually looked like a geranium. But I didn't sign my whole name ~ just my initials. I was getting married the next month, so I signed my first painting with my new initials, SB.

HELLO FIRST PAINTING!
Where have you been all my life?

"Y ou painted that?" Cliff asked when he got home later that day.

"Uh-huh." I felt a little embarrassed about what he might think.

"That's far out! I mean it! You painted that? Wow! It's great! You've been holding out on me!"

"Really?" I could hardly breathe, I was so excited at his words. "You think it looks like a geranium?"

"Oh. Is that what it is?"

He was standing next to me. I exhaled and bumped him with my hip.

"I'm kidding, it's perfect. It's not a good geranium ～ it's a GREAT geranium! You're an artist!" (Huge, gigantic gold star.)

He put his arm around my shoulders and pulled me close, but he never took his eyes off the painting. "Those leaves look real. How'd you know how to do that?" I shook my head at the question because there was no answer. I had no idea. It was an accident.

"I'm going to take it to Doug tomorrow and let him tell you what he thinks!" Doug was the head of the art department at the office, a real artist who sold his work in galleries.

"Are you sure? Really? I don't know."

"He'll love it ～ otherwise I wouldn't bother him."

was beside myself, thrilled because Cliff thought it was good. I knew if he didn't like it, I would see it in his eyes when he tenderly told me, "Never attempt such a thing again." Or he might say, "You really got something there, babe. Why don't you take a few lessons?" But he didn't. If he hadn't been positive, if he'd frowned even the slightest bit, I'm not sure I would have ever painted again ∽ I trusted him more than I trusted myself.

Doug called the next day and was so complimentary. He said the painting was good; he said Cliff told him I'd never had lessons; he said he couldn't believe it was my first try.

I stood there holding the phone, my shoulders hunched up to my ears, almost afraid to hear what he was saying. He called me a natural and said I should keep painting. I got off the phone in awe of him ∽

and me ∽
and the world ∽
and the air ∽
and all living things.

I don't know where my knack for watercolors came from or why it didn't reveal itself earlier. You can see by my childhood art there really is no hint of hidden talent.

SUE   Good

Good?
I think because I understood
the concept of "two."

I thought people were either born with the ability to paint or they weren't. And if they were born with it, I figured they'd be doing it long before they were 30. So it made no sense. All I knew for sure is that it was a gift from God, showing up when it did, like someone leaving surprise flowers on your front porch, but better. It helped me find my way. It changed my life. I can only imagine how many people out there might have hidden talents lurking inside them and not even know it. I am the poster girl for "You don't know unless you try."

From that time on, I couldn't wait to get up in the morning so I could RUN to the kitchen table and open up that beautiful pad of watercolor paper and make my first color mark with the brush. My eraser was to my art what my trusty seam ripper had been to sewing: I could not live without it. It meant I always had a second chance. After a while I realized painting was a lot like making a recipe. I would do my very best because I hated to waste anything; but if worse came to worst and it was horrible, I could throw it away and try again. I wasn't

Renoir ~ I didn't expect to be ~ I didn't even want to be. It didn't seem one bit life changing at the time. It was just a homey little hobby that made me happy.

I bought more colors and a bigger pencil sharpener and painted the things around me, things in my house that I liked. After memorializing my geranium, I did a picture of two little perfume bottles. Then I copied a picture of a yellow cat that was on one of my birthday cards.

For where thy treasure is, there also will thy heart be. ♥

Kitchen Art

I put my SB initials on all of these; but by the time I got to the yellow vase of roses and the basket of pears, I signed my whole name. As I painted more, I got better. Because practice, as in my case, may never make perfect, but it definitely helped.

I took all my "masterpieces" back to Dan at Graham's for framing and hung them all over the walls of my kitchen.

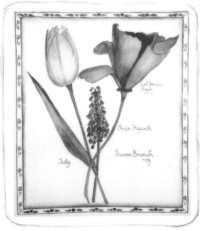

The herdsman & the fairy were married with two gold rings at the parish church. He stayed a herdsman. His fairy wife never gave him the slightest trouble.

♥ FRENCH FOLKTALES

Chapter Eight

I DO, I DO, I DO, I DO, I DO.

The glass house with the silly green fireplace was almost finished. Lots of little details still needed attention, but the basics were there ~ the kitchen, with wood floors, yellow tile counters, and French doors to the backyard, was almost done. The house was at the end of a long drive where we'd planted an orchard of skinny little fruit trees before they even installed the front door.

It's green!

I sat for weeks with my garden books learning which trees would have the juiciest and longest-lasting fruit ~ which varieties of grapefruit, lemons, limes, peaches, figs, and plums kept the longest; which apples were best for cooking, which were best for eating, and which had the prettiest blossoms. I wanted to walk down that long, romantic row of pink-blooming trees I'd seen in the movie *Anne of Green Gables*.

My plan was to hover over those trees: protect them; weed around them; water, feed, and prune them; throw wildflower seed under them; and gratefully harvest from them for the rest of our lives. I had visions of them gnarled and thick with age, their boughs filled with blossoms and fruit.

Peach Blossoms say "I belong to you."

125

Their deepening roots would mirror our own. I dreamed of home-made peach cobbler, sautéed figs and plums, apple crisp, and fresh-squeezed limeade. We would picnic under them in the spring, look up through the branches at the blue sky as pink and white petals fluttered down. We would harvest and be self-sufficient. An orchard like this would make the world a better place.

June 25, 1977

As every fairy tale comes true...

Cliff and I were married under the oaks at the top of the hill in the backyard with all our friends and families in attendance: my grandma, all four of our parents, his brothers, my brothers and sisters, in-laws, cousins, aunts, uncles, best friends, everyone. I felt so proud wearing my English cotton eyelet dress, white macramé espadrilles, and baby's breath in my hair as I walked to the top of the hill behind our new house that lovely sun-splashed morning. Next to me, on the lawn under the oaks, was my handsome, brilliant husband-to-be,

in a beautiful suit. When he took my hand, I felt myself straighten and stand taller. *He's something,* I thought, *There's nothing he can't do; and now, because of him, I'll be something, too.* I turned to look at the faces of everyone I loved. They'd followed us up the hill, handsome men and women in flowery summer dresses, gathered on the lawn in a half circle behind us.

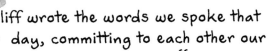 ormally I would almost faint from nervousness in front of a crowd, but not this time. My hands weren't even clammy. I looked at the faces of the people I loved and memorized each one. My mom and Betty were both crying. My dad had his arm around my grandma. Cliff's four-year-old nephew, Ben (wearing a tiny plaid coat and tie), was hanging from the tips of Russ's fingers, standing on his feet and bouncing.

Cliff wrote the words we spoke that day, committing to each other our "lifelong love, understanding, and companionship." I looked straight into his eyes and made sure everyone heard me repeat the words and say, "I do." I felt like I knew what I was doing. (This was a rare feeling, so I took note of it.)

127

After the magic words were spoken, "I now pronounce you man and wife," while our friends and family were clapping and cheering, Cliff bent his head and put his forehead against mine and looked into my eyes. We stayed that way for a moment, eyes locked, time standing still. It was as if our brains mixed together; he took half and I took the other half (apparently I got the good half). We started to laugh. He pulled me to him, kissed my laughing mouth, and we were married.

Darling~ you can count on me
Till the sun dries up the sea
Until then I'll always be
Devoted ~ to you...
♡ Everly Brothers

Our friends made our wedding even more of a fairy tale because almost every card we received had an image of Prince Charming and his Princess Bride going off together on a white horse. I began to refer to Cliff as P.C. (Prince Charming) ~ as in, "Hey, P.C., can you help me bring in the groceries?"

My mom, Russ, me & Cliff

FAMILY PHOTO

After the wedding, we spent the summer finishing the last little bits on the house, choosing wallpaper, getting light fixtures and shoe racks in the closets. It was a funny house because it combined Cliff's taste for modern décor and design, and my love for everything traditional, old-fashioned and cozy. A long wall of mitered glass in the living room looked out over the valley, but in the bedrooms we had old-fashioned New England-type windows with deep sills

for my seashells and vases of flowers. The phone on my side of the bed was white and round with a gold dial and looked like Marilyn Monroe might have owned it. On his side, the phone was fire-engine red, and angular, like a sports car.

129

The old debate about getting a coffee table was revisited. It was a discussion I could not win. He thought they were for old people.

I said, "What do you expect to put your feet on?" thinking of the coffee table in my parents' living room that was almost a member of the family ~ where we put our feet up to watch Ed Sullivan, where we did homework and played slap jack and crazy eights. Every scratch on it was a memory.

He answered, "The couch."

"LESS IS A BORE," wrote Robert Venturi

about modern architecture and design. I could not agree more. Less can be pretty; some could think of it as restful. If you wish to hide your true soul, this is the way to go; because it's a very private sort of decorating. But if you are a heart-on-your-sleeve person, you won't be able to do it. Soon photos of loved ones, quilts, candles, flowers,

Sue -
your eyes sparkle so much -
I thought your ears might as well sparkle too!

Much Love
your friend & husband

P.C. made the card for the earrings he gave me as a wedding present.

130

and treasured books will begin to leak into the picture. Add a teapot or two and it's all over.

DECORATING 101

I would go down to Russell's Coffee Shop with my newest Country Living magazine and eat lunch by myself while I studied the photographs, soaking in every detail on every hutch shelf, the wallpaper behind every dish and cup, the stacks of quilts, the ideas for homemade everything. I read about new recipes and kitchen gardens; picket fences, trellises and arbors; and collecting things like dishes, copper pans, and old baskets. I found out cooking felt even better when I used an old rolling pin or sifter from the thrift store; ones like my mom had when I was growing up.

On the way home I might stop at an antique store and buy an old wicker basket, then fill it with apples,

set it on the table and paint a picture of it. I appliquéd pillows for the sofa just like the ones in the magazine. I leaned on the doorjamb, gazing at my homemade handiwork, smelled the apple crisp cooking in the oven, caressed it all with my eyes, and, mad with house love, kissed the wall.

There are practical little things in housekeeping which no man really understands.
♥ ELEANOR ROOSEVELT

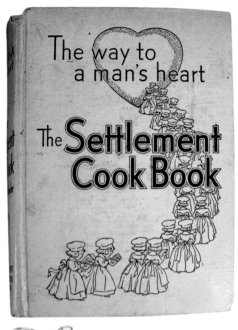

The way to a man's heart

The **Settlement Cook Book**

A Homemade Life

Workmen were always around. I'd be painting at the kitchen table, lost in time, not hearing them, or stuffing pork chops or peeling potatoes, folding clothes or ironing curtains (with that good hot-iron starch smell wafting in the air) ~ while they put knobs on bathroom cupboards, hung the mirror in the guest bath, and painted trim.

When Cliff came home, the house was clean, there were flowers on the table, and his favorite magazines were waiting in the kitchen window seat. I fluted the edge of a piecrust while he inspected finishing touches on the house. We were a team.

The garden-in-progress was filled with handsome young landscapers raking, seeding, and pushing wheelbarrows full of mulch, cement, bricks, or gravel; dragging hoses and trimming dead limbs off trees. I baked cookies for the crew and took them pitchers of ice water and then beers at the end of the day. My girlfriends would stop by to admire the tan, shirtless hunks of masculinity in our yard. It was the good life.

FRIENDS

When I wasn't painting, grocery shopping, cooking, or sewing, I was immersed in garden books. My favorite was a little book published in 1971 called *Betty Crocker's Kitchen Gardens* written by Mary Mason Campbell and illustrated by Tasha Tudor. It was a how-to book, the basic 1-2-3s of home gardening. I learned that when the Pilgrims came, the first thing they did was "plant a few herbs in tiny dooryards with the few cherished seeds they'd brought from home." I wanted to do that, too. A garden was an extension of cooking and the kitchen and of all the things that made home wonderful.

Another inspiring book, *Portrait of a Marriage,* was about an aristocratic couple in 1930s England, Vita Sackville-West and her husband, Sir Harold Nicholson. Together they had a passion for gardening and surrounded their 15th-century manor house with hedges and brick walls that divided spaces into "garden rooms," leaving little gaps and doorways for views into other parts of the garden. Each room was planted with a theme. For example, there was the cottage garden, the rose garden, the sunken garden, and the herb garden ~ and the white garden, filled with tall white flowers, delphiniums, cosmos, roses and bleeding hearts, surrounded with clumps of gray and silver foliage like

Betty Crocker's

KITCHEN GARDENS

A year 'round guide to growing and using herbs and vegetables.
by Mary Mason Campbell
pictures by Tasha Tudor

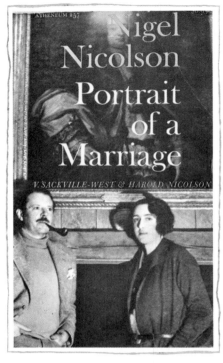

snow in summer and lamb's ears. They had an orchard, too. I dreamed of someday seeing those gardens at Sissinghurst.

Cliff put a small garden just outside the kitchen door, with a dwarf lemon tree in the center. I planted a salad garden ~ short rows of different vegetables, peppers, radishes, and cucumbers. I loved running out to pick a lemon off the tree, some fresh lettuce leaves, herbs, or sun-warmed tomatoes for our dinner. I planted seeds and went outside every morning to watch them grow.

Between the veggies, I planted six-packs of petunias and forget-me-nots for my little vases, and all kinds of fresh herbs. I made basil butter, whipped minced basil into softened butter and kept it in the fridge for eggs and pasta. I did the same with butter and chives for steak and potatoes. I made mint, rose, and lavender sugars for tea. I mixed thyme flowers into softened vanilla ice cream and steeped rosemary and peppercorns in vinegar for salads. I tied up little bunches of herbs and hung them to dry from a shelf in the kitchen. I was a happy Suzy Homemaker trying new things. I always loved the word "wholesome" and that's what this felt like.

I read about soil preparation, compost, companion planting, and double digging. I was learning what you had to do to make plants healthy, what got tied up, what sent out runners, what liked to be planted with what. I wasn't going to be an expert, but I really wanted to be somewhat self-sufficient and provide for our little family of two.

Kitchen garden vegetables are crisp, sweet & filled with good health & well-being.
♥ Mary Mason Campbell

That's what I wanted when I cooked for us and our friends: good health and well-being ~ and flavor. I learned that a juicy, sun-ripened, garden-grown tomato or a freshly dug, garden-grown potato were entirely different creatures than the ones we bought at the supermarket.

Dig warm red potato from garden; wash, leave skin on & immediately drop in boiling water. Cook till soft. Mash in a small dish. Salt. Pepper. Butter. Eat. Die & go to HEAVEN. ♥

Cliff liked working

in the garden, too, but he enjoyed the big jobs: planting hedges and trimming trees. One day he was out for hours cutting branches off the old oaks that overhung the back lawn. He came in looking like he'd rolled in dirt. His yellow T-shirt was filthy and smeared with blood, and a strip of the shirt, at the bottom along the hem, was missing. His belly was showing, and a piece of yellow cloth, obviously ripped from his shirt, was tied around his thumb. There was a little sopped-up blood on it, too. He never looked happier.

"Look at you! What happened? Did you cut yourself?"

He looked at his hand, back at me, eyes getting bigger as he began to see everything through my eyes. Starting to laugh, realizing what he'd done, and already anticipating my reaction, he said, "Oh, it's no big deal. I just skinned my knuckle a little, but it was bleeding so I had to wrap it with something."

I took it in. "Did you use your teeth to tear that piece off your shirt?"

"No," he said, grinning, "I used the chain saw."

"While the shirt was ON you?"

136

"Yes."

Yes? Yes? It would have slowed him down to come inside and wash his hands and bandage his thumb. Instead, while sitting on a tree branch, he pulled out the hem of his filthy T-shirt *while it was on him* and cut off a piece with the chain saw. Total maniac. (I thought maybe I should go get that life insurance policy.) I was just happy he was still in one piece, and went to get the camera.

Reading my garden books, I learned that the "old wives" had left us a wealth of useful, sometimes whimsical information that I took to heart and to the garden.

FOR INSTANCE:

Garlic is GOOD for Roses, repulses Witches; is BAD for Peas. Basil brings NEW LOVE & GROWS better if you SWEAR at it. If you'd LIKE TO BE Married, PUT A Blue BORAGE flower in your lover's tea. When a Ladybug lands on you, Make a Wish. Apple Trees bring Love. Robins are GOOD LUCK.

and more . . .

Tea made from Pansy Leaves, also known as HEARTS-EASE, cures heartbreak.

Chamomile Tea will give you SWEET DREAMS.

Summer Savory is an APHRODISIAC and Sage will keep you young.

Yes, & always be nasty to Nasturtiums.

I learned that some plants & birds made the garden healthier & were natural insect repellents.

FOR EXAMPLE:

TARRAGON expels cabbage moths.

BayLeaves keep

ants out of cupboards.

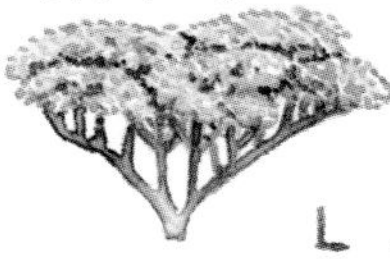

Yarrow attracts
LADYBUGS which eat APHIDS.

Catnip (the beautiful "NEPETA") discourages

MOSQUITOES. A saucer of BEER

will drown slugs & snails.

Hummingbirds love red &

orange flowers & EAT their weight

in GARDEN PESTS. Bees are

attracted to lavender,

sunflowers, nepeta, &

asters. DRAGONFLIES, praying

mantises,  's & GARDEN SNAKES

ARE GOOD for the Garden.

BLUEBIRDS eat beetles Marigolds

prevent whitefly & DISCOURAGE

wild Bunnies.

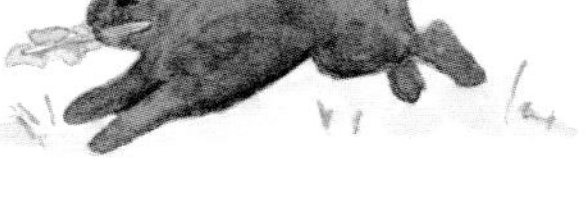

But there seemed nothing we could do about our chief nemesis in the garden: gophers. We had a million of them, and I'm not exaggerating (much). Soaking cotton balls in peppermint oil and dropping them into the holes did not work. I tried that and every other thing to get rid of them.

One day we were expecting company, and I wanted to make the flowerbed around the back deck look extra nice. It was still so new, and it needed color. At the nursery I found several healthy-looking Gerbera plants, each with one, big, bright pink flower at the end of a tall stalk. I brought them home and planted them along the garden path. Finished and back in the house, I admired my handiwork from the kitchen window. I hadn't even washed the dirt off my hands when a big gopher came out from under the deck and took off running next to the path, and almost as if he had clippers, he grabbed every flower by the stalk and dragged them all back under the deck. I stood there, dumbstruck with disbelief, then hopped up and down yelling at him through the glass, but it did no good. He was not afraid of me. He got them all.

The next day I went to the animal shelter to get a cat. I'd never been particularly fond of cats, but I felt I had no choice. The situation was dire. It required the services of a full-time organic exterminator.

140

OH NOOOOO...
Do we have to?

I found a fluffy yellow kitty with round green eyes and a pointed little face, just seven weeks old. I brought her home and named her Pooh.

LOVE LOVE LOVE

She was in our house maybe one day before I was madly, foreverly, without reason, sense, or logic, totally in crazy-love with her. How had I lived so long without a cat!? Not only did she scamper sideways, cuddle next to me, purr in my ear, lie upside-down in my lap, and make me laugh every day, she turned out to be an excellent gopher-hunter. She was worth her weight in gold, but I would have loved her just as much if she never touched a gopher.

My little petty-pet

Have nothing in your house that you do not know to be useful or believe to be beautiful. ♥
WILLIAM MORRIS

Dear Diary

August 1, 1979 – Friday Cliff came home about 4pm last night – + we have this little raft boat that you put air in – it holds 2 – has a motor – and is so neat & comfortable. So I made potatoe salad, roast beef sandwiches, peaches, plums, cookies, iced tea & wine – packed it up – threw the boat in Dick's truck + went to Lake Lopez for the evening. Cliff swam + we ate and talked + were so in love, it was wonderful – We motored back into the lake + were pretty much alone on a glassy beautiful lake – I can't tell you how wonderful it was – we just had so much fun together. All people should be this lucky.

They came to a dear little room & the Prince said to Folly that henceforth this room would be reserved for her. ♥
Folly in Fairyland, Carolyn Wells

CHAPTER NINE
BRANCHING OUT
WITH A LITTLE HELP FROM MY FRIENDS. ♥

My ongoing love affair with watercolors began taking up space. I cleared my art things off the kitchen table every night so that we could eat dinner ～ and brought it all back out in the morning. I liked the kitchen best, it was the center of everything, near the tea and the phone, so I didn't mind.

But after a while Cliff suggested I set up a real studio in his office just off the kitchen. When we built the house he thought he would work there, but as it turned out, he hardly ever used it. My sewing machine had already claimed a corner of it.

It had a long counter that ran beneath small windows that opened out to the garden. I could paint there and still be close to the tea kettle. I wallpapered it in a Marimekko pattern (green stems, red flowers on white background). I could leave my work out and it didn't bother anyone. It was really kind of perfect. It didn't take long before the walls were covered with my paintings.

The summer after we were married, Cliff and I decided it would be fun to have a fashion show in our backyard to help raise money for a project that Cliff's mom had created called Grandmother's House, a nonprofit intergenerational daycare center where young mothers could safely leave their children for a few hours of alone time (or grocery store time or girlfriend time or whatever they needed).

We contacted our favorite clothing stores and asked if they wanted to be involved, and of course they all did.

The stores would provide the clothes and the models, and some of my bravest girlfriends volunteered to model, too. Cliff and I divided up the jobs. Cliff had posters made; we put them in the store windows, and the stores sold tickets to the event. Cliff had his guys set up rows of rented chairs and beach umbrellas on the lawn. Russ got a local winery to donate a free wine bar, servers, and trays of wine glasses. We had outdoor speakers; the music was coordinated to the show, and we had a rehearsal the day before.

My sister, Shelly, was staying with us. She and I cleaned the house and filled it with flowers. We made pitchers of iced tea and pink lemonade, and platters of tea sandwiches, sliced apples and cheese, chocolate-dipped strawberries, and little carrot cupcakes with pink-tinted cream-cheese frosting.

144

The day of the event was perfect. Sunny California clear-blue skies, not too hot ～ roses, lemon blooms and jasmine scented the air. The ladies brought their sisters, moms, and best friends ～ some of them we knew and some we didn't ～ everyone was dressed in their summer best, excited and ready for a party. We turned up the music and filled the wine glasses.

We planned for the models to change in our bedroom, come out through the bedroom doors, strut their stuff three times around the deck so that everyone could see, circle back through the kitchen, down the hall, and back to the bedroom to change into the next outfit ～ and do it again.

When it was time, I quieted everyone down. "All right, ladies, on behalf of Grandmother's House, let the show begin!"

Setting up for the party.

To shrieks and hoots and other expressions of encouragement, the models danced and twirled across the deck to "Stayin' Alive," "How Deep Is Your Love," "Dancing Queen," and "More Than a Woman" in satin tie-tops and palazzo pants, embroidered vests, empire mini-dresses, floaty romantic sundresses, evening trousers, and halter tops. They wore fabulous red boots and silver platform shoes with ankle straps, and some of them wore heart-shaped sunglasses. They carried beach balls, transistor

radios, straw bags, and fringed purses. It was a Disco Inferno out there. Annie Hall had just come out, so there were big hats and baggy pants with vests and men's ties. Everyone was on their feet, dancing, cheering and clapping.

The best was saved for last. For the grand finale, the shop that sold fur coats had combined forces with a lingerie boutique. The models came out wearing huge sunglasses and spun across the deck in gorgeous fur coats and high heels (this is way back when, before we understood that fur coats cost something, and not just money). When the models slid the furs off their shoulders, or turned quickly and opened their coats, the audience saw flashes of long pearls and lots of skin decked out in pink satin teddies and tap pants, yellow chiffon peignoirs, bridal corsets laced with blue-satin ribbons, mink-edged bustiers with garters and black net stockings. Whistles, applause, shouts, and screams of laughter rang out.

Although this party had been advertised for women, the word had gone out. Husbands and boyfriends had leaked in through the back gate and were hanging over the fence watching the show. You could hear the cheers, the hoots, and hollering for miles over the valley. It was a wonderful show. Nobody wanted it to end, and we made lots of money for Grandmother's House.

Something else happened that day. People were in and out of the house all afternoon. I didn't realize it, but many of them stopped by my studio art room and saw my paintings. Cliff brought people in, and so did Betty, Elaine, and Diana. People ~ even ones I didn't know ~ began coming up, complimenting my art and asking where I showed my paintings. It was totally unexpected. I was just painting for my house to match my decorating. Now people were asking if they could buy them. By the time the party was over, three of my paintings were spoken for. I was stunned. I could barely sleep that night, replaying the entire wonderful day in my mind.

I can live for two months on a good compliment. ♡ Mark Twain

The next week I received several calls asking about my paintings from people who had been at the party. The fact that strangers wanted my art opened a whole new world for me. This was so much better than the pillows! Painting was something of my own that I could do at home, something Cliff approved of. He was proud. He gave me a Polaroid camera and said, "Be sure to take pictures of your paintings before you give them away." And I did. I put the Polaroids in a little red scrapbook.

Original Watercolors
by
Susan Branch

...and painted my first "business card."

My book of watercolors

hen something else surprising happened. I had a close girlfriend named Jane who was a few years older than me. Jane and I met through her boyfriend, David, a business partner of Cliff's. They lived in Marin County, north of San Francisco, where she was the right-hand person to George Lucas. She and David even lived in the house where George (I called him that because she did) wrote *Star Wars*. They would come to our house for the weekend sometimes.

would cook for them and hang out with Jane while the boys had their meetings. She laughed when I told her how much I looked up to her, but she was the perfect role model: a glamorous, independent, funny, creative, confident businesswoman with

silky straight brown hair down to her rear end who told stories in her soft drawl about meeting Elvis Presley when she was 14 and he was 19. Everyone loved her. She had a cat she called Goosie, and she enjoyed keeping house just as much as I did. I had huge bowls of oranges in my kitchen and made fresh-squeezed juice in the morning, because that's what Jane did at her house.

hen Jane married David in 1978, I made them a recipe box for a wedding present. I filled an old wooden file box with recipe cards I'd watercolored with borders, bowls, and baskets. On each card I wrote a favorite recipe in long-hand. Jane loved it. She also insisted on buying several of

my first paintings for her house, which I consided the supreme compliment.

One night, Jane and I were in my kitchen, talking and laughing while making dinner. The boys were out in the hot tub. I was stuffing homemade toasted breadcrumbs mixed with olive oil, garlic, Parmesan cheese, parsley, and basil into hollowed-out tomatoes. The house smelled wonderful, Pooh wove in and out between our legs, Frank was singing, "Only five minutes more . . ."

The oven-timer went off, and I danced the bowl and spoon over to Jane.

"Here, will you stuff the rest of the tomatoes so I can baste the chicken?"

She started spooning the breadcrumb mixture into the tomatoes. "This smells so good. Sue, you are such a good cook ~ you should write a cookbook."

Jane's recipe box

"Right," I said, thinking she was just being nice, while turning the roasting pan, basting, and smiling at the thought.

"No! I mean it! You could do a book just like the recipe cards you did for me."

"You mean with watercolors?"

"Yes, people would love a whole book of that. Do the little illustrations; paint those borders and little bowls. Everything you make is delicious. Use all your recipes and do it just like you did my recipe cards."

"Jane, I can't write a book. I wouldn't know where to start."

"People do it all the time. You could, too. Why not? You should!"

I gave her the "You're crazy" look ~ I never saw people "do it all the time." I never saw anyone do it.

The music changed or the guys came in from the hot tub, and that was the end of the subject. But the thought filed itself in the way-back recesses of my mind ~ a tiny seed, that, despite no encouragement at all (from me), took root anyway and began to grow . . . but really slowly, imperceptibly.

It's easy to look back now and say: Why weren't you more confident? But the truth is, I just wasn't. Believing in myself was probably the hardest thing I ever had to learn to do.

Of course I was flattered, because it was Jane who suggested it, but me? Write a book? Regular people didn't write books in 1979. Margaret Mitchell wrote books, Jane Austen, Julia Child, Harper Lee. Brilliant people, not normal people. Whenever it crossed my mind, which was rare, I was quick to rule it out as an option by reminding myself that I wasn't Louisa May Alcott or John Steinbeck, and that's who wrote books.

I just liked to cook & feed people.

Then Elaine convinced me to let her take two of my paintings with her on a trip to LA; she was going to stop at the Staircase Gallery in Beverly Hills to see if they might be interested. The gallery took them both on consignment, and they sold. I learned that Walter Matthau had purchased my painting of a basket filled with African violets.

Despite the interest, and the fact that an actual movie star had bought one of my paintings, I still thought of it as a hobby. Being a wife was my real job ~ everything I did, whether cooking, gardening, or painting, was part of homemaking, not something that was "going" anywhere, and certainly not a career. I wasn't an artist. This sudden interest in my paintings was obviously a fluke. Soon people would wake up, smell the flowers, and not buy my art anymore. I couldn't understand why they were buying my pictures in the first place.

It's funny: I'd wished for a miracle like this to happen, and when it did, I didn't recognize it. I jumped right into denial mode. I just could not believe it. It was like trying on a ball dress when you *know* you're not the ball dress type and you LOVE it, but no matter how good it looks on you, you still feel funny in it, so you only wear it around the house.

Me on Kauai

I brought my sketchbook, brushes, and watercolors with me when Cliff and I went to Hawaii for a vacation with our friends.

I put my art things away when we went to dirt bike races. I was too worried watching Cliff try to break his other shoulder to sketch ~ and wondering how anyone could stand to eat that much dirt.

152

I loved the car shows we attended. I'd leave Cliff swooning in ecstasy in the Italian sports car department and go look at the old cars. I was the exact opposite of Cliff when it came to cars. I thought they should have stopped changing the designs in the 1950s. Up to then, they were perfect. Each had a distinctive personality and

tons of style, like pieces of art. You could tell them apart, and you had a choice for everything you needed: pink Cadillacs for the rock and roll guys, '57 Chevys for date night, '59 T-bird convertibles for the beach, and a lovely assortment of winged station wagons for the family. They had great radios; the seats were long benches, as comfortable as living room sofas and heaven for the drive-in.

What else could anyone want? Three people fit in the front seat. Who needed a console? The height of wonderfulness was when you were the girl between two guys, windows down, *Little Latin Lupe Lu* coming from the radio. We all wanted to be that girl.

153

FALLING IN LOVE WITH NATURE

I got in the habit of walking around the golf course at the bottom of our hill early every morning before the golfers came out, when it was quiet ~ I can still hear the chic-chic-chic of the huge commercial sprinklers fanning over the expanse of perfect green, smell the mowed grass, see the shimmer of the water drops cascading in the sun through the eucalyptus trees, hear the whistle of the train winding through the valley.

· · · · · · · · · · · · · · · S A N   L U I S   O B I S P O · · · · · · · · · · · ·

Some days I would hike up Madonna Mountain, a long-extinct volcanic peak that juts up in the middle of town. I'd climb a thousand feet on the dusty trail, up the steep, scrub-oak-covered mountain where hummingbirds zipped and bees buzzed in the ceonothus; where clumps of California poppies, Indian paintbrush, and morning glories clambered around rocks and streamed down the hillside, and the smell of sun-warmed sage-brush filled the air. Sweeping 360-degree views of the town, hills, and valleys, all the way to the sea, were the breathtaking reward for the climb.

"Come walk with me," I said to Cliff (all the time). "You'll love it up there. It's gorgeous."

"You know I'm not going to do that. Why don't you give up? You already know the answer. I'm not a walker. I'm not a tennis player and I'm not a camper. I'm none of those things you want me to be."

"Why not? Walking is such good exercise ~ and it's beautiful. You would love the view. I don't think it would kill you to walk with me."

"Yes, it would. It would kill me."

"It's not just walking, you know. It's us. Time together. We can talk."

"We talk. You think we don't talk? We talk constantly. What we really need is time not to talk."

Shelly on our walk.

I would get Diana or Sarah or my sister, and we would talk the whole way and try to figure out what was wrong with men. Thank GOD for girlfriends, we said.

Sometimes I wonder if men & women really suit each other. Perhaps they should live next door & just visit now & then.
Katharine Hepburn

One day I called my grandma to get her recipe for nut bread (which, she liked to say, "wasn't just for nuts").
We were talking about the family, about my brothers and sisters, about life, love, and marriage. I asked her if men were the same in her day as they were in ours . . . mostly only

My grandfather, Willard Smith, man-about town, bon vivant in his pilot hat, was a bite my grandma found too big to chew.

interested in man things. She said yes, she thought they were about the same ~ "but women don't pay attention." She told me she'd realized with my grandfather that women "should pay less attention to what men say, and watch what they do." She said this worked with all people, but especially boyfriends, husbands, and politicians. I thought it sounded important, my grandma was very smart; I filed it in the back of my mind to mull over later.

As our marriage went on, I could see that Cliff really didn't like sentimentality of any kind. We argued about the value of my photo albums. He would ask, "Why do you bother?" I kept making them, saving all our photos and mementos; I was sure he'd want them someday. He thought I lived in the past. He did not like Christmas; he didn't like my old music, couldn't see the purpose in my scrapbooks or my diary ~ especially my diary. He thought my Beatrix Potter people were "junk." He'd notice them every so often and say, "Why do we have these?"

DIANA & ME

Take care of all your memories, for you cannot relive them. ♥ Bob Dylan

156

When things like that happened, it was confusing. Why didn't we agree? I was not putting two and two together. We were in love, but we had different ideas. I took him to the airport for a business trip, and when I came home I found the note he left: "Cross your fingers for me up in that little plane, so I can get home and give you all my love. I miss you already, Cliffy." "Cliffy." Sigh.

D E A R   D I A R Y

Oct 27 1979 Sat. Cliff just took off in his hot air balloon — I woke at 7:15 and thought "Oh No, it must be too foggy — they aren't coming" and then I heard the sound of the hot air — & said "Cliff your B'day surprise is outside — Listen" — and he jumped & leaped & got so excited & was dressed in 5 min — I can't even write how exciting it is to have a HUGE orange balloon out in the front yard — and how neat it is to finally give him a present he LOVES! I feel great! so now I've got to get busy with breakfast — What a terrific day so far!

While he was floating high over the valley, I made a pancakes-and-bacon birthday breakfast with cantaloupe halves filled with vanilla ice cream for our friends who were there waiting when he returned, triumphant, from his adventure. We ate under blue skies on the deck next to the garden at the bottom of the green grassy hill where we'd been married.

The summer seems like it will Dream on FOREVER.
♥ Elizabeth von Arnim

Every week I had "Tuesday Girls" at my house. All my best friends would gather around my kitchen table, drink tea, teach each other things and have girl talk, commonsensically solving all the world's problems every time we were together.

COMMON SENSE IS INSTINCT, ENOUGH of IT IS GENIUS.
George Bernard Shaw

The house rang with laughter as we shared craft ideas, recipes, beauty tricks, and handy household tips. We also kept one eye on the TV so we wouldn't miss anything Luke and Laura might be up to on General Hospital.

I told them what my grandma said about "Watch what people do, don't listen to what they say." We hashed it over, nodding in recognition, and decided my grandma was a genius.

Timeless Tips
from the Tuesday Girls
It's a Girl Thing

...cuteness counts...

In a Bloating Emergency, resulting in a too-tight waistband, hook a rubberband through your buttonhole and around button.

Mini marshmellows or Life Savers make good birthday-candle holders.

Protein **M**ask for hair: Take a handful of "real" mayonnaise and rub it into your hair, coating every strand. Wrap your head in plastic wrap and leave it on for half an hour.

In a pinch, masking tape works to hem pants.

Add mint to bouquets of roses for extra fragrance.

Tuesday Girls **E**ye **D**e-**P**uff: If you've been crying and your eyes are swollen, lie down, put one cold, wet (used) tea bag (not herb tea) on each eye, and leave in place for 10 minutes.

remove the string

Itchy skin or Sunburn? Put a cup of soothing oats in your bath.

NOODLES

Use cold water to soak starchy pans, where you've cooked pasta, rice, cereal or potatoes.

Fastest way to stop procrastinating about cleaning your house is to send out invitations to a party.

YOU'RE
INVITED

159

For a few months, Liz taught us how to quilt by hand. While we worked on our quilt squares, I taught everyone how to speak "Arf and Arfy" (the secret language my mom learned from Little Orphan Annie comics when she was a kid). It was a handy thing to know when you were talking on the phone but not alone.

BLANKET STITCH

BRING THREAD THROUGH FABRIC AT A, HOLD THREAD W/ THUMB; GO DOWN AT B AND UP AT C, WITH NEEDLE OVER THREAD— PULL INTO PLACE. USE THE RUNNING STITCH TO EMBROIDER YOUR NAME & THE DATE ON YOUR PROJECT.

We blew eggs and decorated them at Easter and went caroling at Christmas. Janet showed us how to make padded, heart-shaped fabric photo frames; I taught embroidery; Jeanie taught knitting; and while Sarah showed us how to macramé bracelets with beads, I gave a cooking class ~ how to make linguini in clam sauce and my dad's garlic bread.

Then it was Diana's Day ~ she taught us how to make margaritas with freshly-squeezed grapefruit juice, salted glasses, and fresh limes. Then she required we go out back, turn up the music, lie in the sun, and drink them.

¼ c. fresh squeezed pink grapefruit juice
¼ c. white tequila
¼ c. triple sec
2 T. frozen limeade concentrate
½ tsp. Grenadine

FILL GLASS WITH CRUSHED ICE. MIX INGREDIENTS IN SHAKER. POUR OVER ICE. ADD LIME & GRAPEFRUIT SLICES AS GARNISH.

Serves One

Diana's Margarita

We all agreed we loved Diana's day best of all ~ from then on every Tuesday was Diana's Day.

160

We were known to burst into song out there on the deck. When Leslie Gore chanted "You don't own me," we knew all the words and everyone sang along: ". . . Don't say I can't go with other boys . . ."

♪ And DON'T TELL ME WHAT TO DO . . . ♪

I always got the girls out of the house before Cliff came home. He did not like having a bunch of women in his castle at the end of his workday, especially (God help us) if they were singing, and ESPECIALLY if they were singing "You Don't Own Me."

At Diana's house, Paul didn't like it if I was there with Diana when he came home, and neither did any of my other girl-friends' boyfriends and husbands, so it seemed normal. They thought we were a bad influence on each other, probably because we all knew how to speak Arf and Arfy and they didn't. It was a little unnerving and hard to understand, but my dad hadn't been par-ticularly thrilled when my mom's friends were over either, so we just mimicked our mothers, tried not to put it in their faces, and did what we wanted to. It was the way of the world.

It's so easy to be wicked without knowing it, isn't it? ♥ L.M. Montgomery

That's why when Billy Joel sang, I love you "just the way you are," there wasn't a dry female eye in the house.

Because were starting to think they really *didn't* like us the way we were. Now that we were all 16 years past 12, we found out they much preferred us to behave like female impersonators: kinda dumb, a little blind, light on opinions, with tight clothes.

♪ Don't go changin' to try & please me... ♫

I think this growing misunderstanding between men and women affected my parents' marriage, too, because when I was 28, they got divorced. My mom, quite innocently, needed to stretch her wings (at least she needed to think she could if she wanted to); and my dad held tighter than ever for fear of losing her. We all know how hard a divorce is on the young children of a couple who are breaking up. It was awful for my younger sisters, but 28, for me, wasn't that great, either.

Grow up, fall in love, get a
little house, plant some
roses, get a kitty, live
happily ever after.
What could be more simple?
Every movie had it in it.

162

CHAPTER TEN
The State of the Union

Courage, dear heart.

C. S. Lewis

Then Lena said to Foundling, "If you won't forsake me, I won't forsake you."
"Never, ever," said Foundling.

Grimm's Fairytales

Even though my mom lived just a three-hour drive away, we wrote letters back and forth constantly. Long-distance phone calls were expensive, so letters were the regular way to communicate. Everyone wrote long letters, three and four pages, almost always in their own handwriting (and, I have to say, we miss them out here in the future). My mom sent me things with her letters: photos, recipes, and articles she'd cut out of the paper.

Still tucked into my diary is a clipping she sent a year after Cliff and I were married, a little poem called "Babies." (Uh-oh, I thought when I saw it, and I was right. Get ready):

"We've planned for babies later on,"
You hear young couples sigh.
"First we must get a home and car . . .
Then children bye and bye."
And so they spurn God's greatest gift –
Small angels from above –

While all around them other homes
Are blessed with children's love.
It takes a lot to raise a child
These days, we all agree . . .
They're precious things - expensive, too -
But what a luxury!
Nick Kenny, 1959

Do you think she was trying to tell me something? (I give my mom credit that in my whole life, this was ALL she ever said about the subject, my mom never interfered or even gave her opinion unless I asked her ∼ and I know she thought long and hard before she sent that poem.)

Me at 12, my newest sister
Mary, & her big sister, Paula.

I'd seen up close how difficult and demanding it was to raise children when I was growing up as the oldest of eight. I was not spurning "God's greatest gift" but I understood what kind of commitment it took. And as far as I was concerned, if you were married, having a baby was a joint decision. Both people had to want it. Babies should be the center of the universe; both parents needed to be thrilled, excited, and wildly involved. You can't have some- one standing in the corner pouting while you're trying to take care of a baby.

I wasn't going to try and do this if Cliff didn't want to ～ although I assumed he would want a baby someday. But so far, he wasn't interested: He brought home a bumper sticker: "Control Your Local Stork." He said the world was already too crowded and quoted statistics about population growth and used the word "billions," which was much more than I thought we were talking about. I was only talking about one little baby. But at this point, he even thought getting another kitty was too much. Too much domestication was going on.

So I thought, I'll just wait. He's younger than me. He'll grow into the idea over time. Doesn't everyone? Isn't that what people DO?

♪ True love means planning a life for two,
Being together the whole day through...
True love means waiting & hoping that soon,
Wishes we've made will come true... ♪
♥ RAY HILDEBRAND... Hey Paula

Cliff had just turned 30 and was, as ever, totally absorbed in his businesses, still going a million miles a minute, and traveling a lot. Sometimes I went along, but more and more, because he was usually busy with appointments, and because I never loved flying unless it was for a good reason, I often stayed home.

He and Tom had sold Stereo West and Warehouse Sound to CBS Corporation. Tom went off to race cars professionally, and Cliff started a hot tub business called California Cooperage. He was under a lot of pressure, getting it off the ground meant building a new warehouse and long hours. Plus he'd branched out and started his own advertising agency.

My "pressures" were harder to see and more personal, and I had the sense that I didn't deserve to have them. Sometimes people would say to me, "What do you DO all day?" in a way that made me know they thought I was a pampered do-nothing Stepford Wife. It would stop me cold, because when I thought about it, they were right, I had no idea what I did all day. One thing I did, and that person didn't, was mind my own business . . . but other than that, I made things. I painted. I didn't keep track. I did laundry, fixed dinner, weeded the garden, vacuumed, and kept the house clean; I went to the grocery store, the butcher, and the fish market. I washed lettuce, and polished my pots and pans. What was I supposed to do?

Hearing something like that made me feel worthless. I wasn't the only one who felt that way. It was 1980, and many of my girlfriends who were stay-at-home wives and moms were questioning the order of things. Sometimes we felt like what we did didn't matter, it wasn't enough. We talked about the idea of contributing, "finding our purpose," but we didn't know how. Our mothers had, for the

most part, stayed home with the children (and, in some cases, became like one of them, under the dominion of the bread-winner). But we were being encouraged by the culture and the changing times to get out there, express our needs and follow our dreams. Now all we had to do was figure out what our needs and dreams were. For a lot of us this was unexplored territory.

I L♥VE YOU.
YOU'RE PERFECT.
(NOW CHANGE.)

Our guys couldn't help. They didn't understand; how could they if we didn't? We would try to talk to them about it, but it was threatening, a "problem" they couldn't solve. Here they had "given" us everything, and we "weren't happy."

Me, too. I felt guilty because (a) I had it all, and (b) I did nothing to deserve it. When I would try and explain it to Cliff, he would say I was spoiled, which was hard to hear. I didn't feel spoiled, I felt like a burden. I thought I was doing what he wanted me to do. Sticking up for myself, the thing he liked about me when he hired me to work at Stereo West, had lost its charm. At this point, three years into our marriage, I was completely dependent on him both emotionally and financially. If I ever imagined I was, or could be, independent, that thought was gone. I hadn't even noticed it going.

*E*ven Diana, who had a wonderful calling as a neonatal nurse ~ Paul wanted her to quit her job, stay home, take care of the house and him. He offered to pay her to quit. He said he'd put a year's salary in her bank account so that she'd feel secure. She was thinking about doing it, because she wanted a baby. But she loved her job, and he wasn't asking her to marry him; and she didn't know if she could juggle having a baby and being a nurse at the same time. Not to mention the fact that Paul wasn't wild about having a baby. It was all such a mess. None of us knew what we were doing and it made us restless.

*W*e couldn't see it then, but we were in the process of creating something new. We were the reluctant and naïve Lewises and Clarks of the women's movement, the ones in the trenches, and it was all uncharted territory.

We were not Playboy Bunnies turned feminists forging a career by writing about it; we were not burning our bras for the newspapers. We were the normal, everyday people, trying to cope, both women and men. We had to carve trails through unfamiliar terrain and trudge through snake-infested swamps to find our way. It wasn't a matter of jumping on the bandwagon; it was a matter of being run over by it.

*G*loria Steinem said, "A woman has two choices: either she's a feminist or a masochist." I could see the truth in that. I knew what I was supposed to want, but wanting it left me feeling dissatisfied and guilty. Not having it made me feel like nothing, and I had no idea how to go about getting it, whatever it was. I had this yearning inside, to do something, to be something, but no idea what or how.

I feel an earnest & humble desire, & shall do till I die, to increase the stock of harmless cheerfulness. ♥ Charles Dickens

I didn't get it that we were evolving; like on a runaway train where there was no getting off. The only thing I thought I knew about evolution was that maybe someday people would be born without appendixes or baby toes. Everything else, I imagined, was a choice.

In the books I loved, my heroes like Scarlett O'Hara and Jo March made their own ways. And they lived in much tougher times than these, woman-wise that is. Of course, they weren't real.

And though I'd been selling one or two paintings a month for three years and brought in enough money to pay for my art supplies, it never occurred to me that I could make a living at it. I never saw it as a "career." Painting was just a cute girly hobby like almost everything I did. I figured if I could do it, anyone could. Self-esteem wasn't as common then as it is today. As soon as I heard about it, I set my mind on getting some; but it didn't come until later.

My entire identity was built on the foundation of my husband. (Yes, I know, but it was a different time.) He was still the be-all and end-all of my life, the embodiment of my childhood dreams, the fairy-tale Prince Charming. They said, "Hitch your wagon to a star," and I'd certainly gotten that part right. It's just that real life was a bit more complicated than a child's dream.

There was also this twisted logic rattling around in the pea brains of these guys of ours: because they had given us "everything," they felt they had the right to do anything they pleased. Like, I'm inviting you out to dinner, so now you owe me. Not all guys, but some. Ones I knew. Great guys in many ways, but engaged in rationalization and deception, self and otherwise. Entitled. It didn't feel right, but at the time it was still hard to put a finger on it, and it didn't matter anyway, there wasn't much we could do about it, since we had fallen in love with them.

In the 70s and early 80s we were breaking new ground, but some of what was being dug up should have stayed buried.

I have not the pleasure of understanding you. ♥ *Jane Austen*

I just wrote everything down . . .

April 4, 1980 OK. Here's the thing,
I think would make a real better life:
1. Get another Kitty for Pooh
2. Make the perfect garden
3. Be a real artist
4. Start a restaurant — a lunch restaurant —
for my girlfriends — open from 1 – 5 & tea at 4.
OR have a knitting-embroidery store so
every day can be Tuesday Owls!
5. Have a baby + take her to the store
6. Work for Country Living Magazine!!!
7. See if Cliff would move to New England
   for a year

Dear Diary...

June 2, 1980 Cliff's in NY so I have the house
to myself. On the stereo is Tommy Dorsey's
band with F. Sinatra singing "Whenever it's
early twilight through twilight I watch till a
star breaks through, funny it's not a star I
see — it's always you." ♡ I'm staying home
tonight, just me, Frank, Pooh - reading my
new book "Zelda" all about Zelda Fitzgerald
(wife of F. Scott). & writing in YOU, dear diary.
I've got mayo in my hair, lemon juice on
my nails, & I'm giving myself a facial
with steam + chamomile flowers from
the garden. Now I ask you — what
could ask for anything more !!! ?

171

Then a weasel or some other creature flashed past ahead of them.

The fairy bowed her head because, as everyone knows, that's not a good sign.

French Fairy Tales

Chapter Eleven

JUST MY IMAGINATION

Love is a fire. But whether it's going to warm your hearth or burn down your house, you never can tell. ♥ *Joan Crawford*

Things began to change at our house. Cliff was home less, and more distant when he was. Sometimes I felt like he didn't want me around. It was like he'd hung a closed sign on the door to his heart. I asked if there was something wrong. He assured me it was just work. His words were soothing (ish), but his actions definitely weren't.

For one thing, he didn't want to go anywhere anymore, not with me anyway. I resisted my natural inclination toward interrogation and tried not to ask him where he'd been, or why he was late, because if I did, he'd say I didn't trust him, or that it's just my imagination. It got so bad, I might have taken a peek at our credit card statements to get a better lay of the land, but all our bills went directly to the office. I hoped this was just a bump in the road and all would go back to normal soon. I tried to be supportive, and kept busy with the house ~ I had an idea of painting a bunny on the wall in the front hall and was occupied with that. Everything would be fine and sometimes not knowing is be better than knowing.

But things continued to deteriorate; nothing I did made him happy. Even his favorite chicken stuffed with cheese didn't cheer him up. The only way I could get his attention was by standing in front of the TV. It was wearing on me ~ he didn't seem to like me and to tell you the truth, I was beginning not to like him either.

173

I started thinking about what my grandmother said: I stopped listening to his crazy-making assurances and watched what he was doing.

MY DIARY

MISERY and the funny thing is he thinks I'm afraid he'll leave, but the real truth is lately I'm more afraid I'll leave.

It felt sudden, but it really wasn't. It just seemed that way because I'd chosen, once again, to put my head in the sand. Within a year, in a string of happenings too trite and one-sided and sadly predictable to drag everyone through, I realized that Cliff's old pattern had come back to haunt us and everything I held dear about love and life was swept away in a maelstrom of confusion, anger, and blame. No one said "paradise" when answering the phone and there were no more gold stars.

There's something n a s t y in the wood shed.
Stella Gibbons COLD COMFORT FARM

My husband didn't love me. Actually, what he said was that he loved me, he just wasn't IN love with me. And, in fact, the whole "marriage thing" wasn't for him. And, there was something else ~ actually, someone else. I stood at the living room window tearfully watching his car speed down the driveway. He didn't want to talk about it.

I was crushed. My heart broke into a thousand pieces. I didn't know what to do. You've been through this before, I berated myself, you should have known better, you should have known sooner. I should have, but I didn't. And this time the hurt carried a much sharper sting being married-hurt and all.

Despite my humiliation and shock at the betrayal, I didn't run right out the door. I held on for a little while longer while the slow painful unveiling of his misdemeanors began to add up. I wanted to turn back time, wave a magic wand and figure out how to make it right. I hoped we could go to marriage counseling, but he said I could forget about any of that female psychobabble mumbo-jumbo ~ if that's what I wanted, I could do it alone. I told him I was going to tell his mother.

Because, if it was truly over, then what? Who was I without "us?" No one. I felt like the ground was dropping out from under me.

I woke one morning at 2 a.m. and, as usual, he wasn't there. I crawled out of bed because I was freezing, my heart was beating a hundred miles a minute, I was sure I was having a heart attack. I took Pooh and went to the kitchen and called the emergency room at the hospital and told them my symptoms. The person on the phone suggested I breathe into a paper bag because she thought I was having an anxiety attack.

I'd never heard of an anxiety attack. But it seems that's what can happen when you live a lie.

EXPERIENCE: that most brutal of teachers. But you do learn, my God do you learn. C. S. Lewis

iserable days passed. Cliff hardly came home; when he did he was inaccessible and cold and he didn't want to talk. He wanted what he wanted, and he wasn't going to let any kind of emotion get in the way, not his (guilt) and certainly not mine (despair).

It had always worked like this. He never left. He would just be mean and act like nothing mattered until I couldn't take it anymore. Now, I had to choose: I could hope the situation would change, stay and feel like nothing ~ And probably it would happen again.

Or, I could go. Say goodbye to the last 10 years of my life. If I went, what would be my future? It would be nothing, too. I could visualize nothing. I had not planned for this. I went round and round, caught in a trap between two nothings.

Her mind was all disorder. The past, present, future, everything was terrible.
Jane Austen

y mother's voice was in my ear: "You know right from wrong." I steadied myself. There was really no choice. I stayed until I mustered the strength to deal with it; and then I finished myself off because I left.

In the fall of 1981, I rented a partially furnished two-bedroom ranch house in a neighborhood over by the high school, moved out and took my Pooh kitty with me. My sister Shelly, who was now twenty,

176

brought over her stuff and moved in with me so I didn't have to be alone. I put my cookbooks in the kitchen and hung my clothes in the closet, put my diary next to the bed. After a couple of days, I went out and bought a coffee table.

I am woman hear me roar...

It was good having my sister there, but she was almost as sad as me. Shelly believed in forever, too. After the divorce of our parents, this was still another impossible unraveling in her young life. There was a lot of this kind of collateral damage. It wasn't just Shelly and I who believed in fairy tales. No one wants their friends to break up, it sort of ruins everything.

Goodbye, yellow brick road...

At first I thought I was managing. In the back of my mind, I was sure Cliff would come to his senses. Once he saw I was really gone, he'd show up at my door, all contrite ~ it could happen any minute now. While I waited, I ruminated on whether I should take him back. I just couldn't decide. Tra-la, tra-la.

In the meantime, I tried to act normally, show a happy face, and hide my grief as best I could. I went to the movies and had lunches with my girlfriends and lived in a kind of limbo, stuck between the past and the future. Every day was worse than the day before as it began to sink in that Cliff was not coming to get me. Rejection is a terrible thing. You feel unloved, unwanted, and worthless.

REJECTED

Ticking Clock, *tedious, ad nauseam, tear-stained sadness,* tick-tock, tick-tock...
I'm Sorry.

I hoped time would make things better, but instead insult was added to injury. It took him about 15 minutes to bring that home wrecker to live in my house, with my kitchen, my green fireplace, my lemon tree, my stuff. This person had slipped into my spot and was now a squatter in my house while most of my clothes were still hanging in the closet. I was as replaceable as a lightbulb.

About a month after I moved out, I called Cliff to ask if I could go by the house and pick up a few more of my things (I was still asking his permission ～ why, I do not know), preferably at a time that girl wouldn't be there (oh yeah, that's why).

I found some of my clothes on the floor; hard to believe, she had the nerve to wear them. But actually, worse, she'd been using my personal, private Erno Lazlo black face soap! Her touching that soap upset me more than her being with Cliff. I mean really. It was disgusting, wearing my clothes, using my things, living in my house. I apologized to the house ～ I am so sorry I left you with these people. I worried about the unfinished bunny I'd drawn on the wall in the front hall. I supposed Cliff would just paint over it.

bye - bye bunny

The paperback lying open and flat on the table next to "her side of the bed" (next to my Marilyn Monroe telephone) was the kind you get at a gas station, with a lightening storm and a half-naked woman on the cover, called *The Creeping Terror*. How could he like her? I was surprised; from what I'd heard, I didn't think she could read. Diana referred to her as "Dimmi."

I got a brown grocery bag from where we kept them next to the fridge. The kitchen was a mess: dirty dishes, food stuck to my yellow tile counters, an open pizza box still had pizza in it. I gathered up my soap and makeup, my Shalimar and Chanel No. 5, my Calvin Klein jeans and my wildflower bubble bath and put them in the bag to take with me. I unplugged my phone and put it in the bag; then I ripped out the last two pages of her book and threw them in too (I would have died if this happened to me; it was the one bright light in an otherwise miserable day). I'd been putting it off, but now I realized I was going to have to get everything out of there, ASAP.

By Christmas I was face down on the sofa, unable to go anywhere because I could no longer mask the pain of being the last-to-know moron-wife deserted by her husband for a 20-year-old girl. For all practical purposes, I'd aged from 33 to 50 overnight. I couldn't bear to have anyone see me.

MINE ENEMY IS GRIEF...ONE OF US MUST DIE. ♥ PROCTER,1858

Nothing is sadder than a pathetic, stringy-haired, over-the-hill girl in the same wrinkled flannel jammies and old sweater she's worn for a week, in a darkened room in the middle of the day, hunched over a coffee table drinking white wine out of a coffee mug with permanent couch cushion creases pressed into her swollen, tear-stained cheeks.

179

I looked around the room through slits-for-eyes, the TV flickering in the corner, the theme music from Days of Our Lives playing, liver-colored shag carpeting and olive-green plaid drapes (not my fault, they came with the house), pulled shades throwing dirty yellow light on the undecorated Christmas tree hulking darkly in the corner, all ugly. The TV was relentless, "Like the sands through the hourglass, so are the days of our lives." Oh God. I burst into fresh tears and dug through the sofa cushions looking for the remote.

> My life is a perfect graveyard of buried hopes. L.M. Montgomery

Diana came by and heard me sobbing. She pounded on the door, saying, "You let me in this minute." And then she saved my life.

"What are you doing? What are you watching?" She found the remote and snapped off the TV. "It's disgusting in here." She left the door open; a fresh breeze blew in and crashed into the gloom.

"When was the last time there was any air in this house?" She hustled around pulling up shades, opening windows. "You even managed to kill off the pine smell from the Christmas tree."

"I think I used up the air a couple days ago." Mumbling, head in hands, squinty eyes looked up at her, "I've been dead ever since."

"How about light? People can't live in the dark!" She turned to me. "Get up. You know it's animal cruelty making Pooh live like this? I could report you to the SPCA. Up!"

"OK, I'm up." The light hurt. I went to the kitchen and put on sunglasses. They perked the outfit right up.

"Have you looked in the mirror lately? Where's Shelly? Does she know what you're doing?"

"She's at work."

Pooh was sad too.

"Go take a shower, sweetie. You'll feel so much better if you wash your hair and put some sweet-smelling lotion on yourself. Let's get you up and clean and go have lunch at the beach! It's my day off! You can't go on like this. Gimme those." She pulled off my sun-glasses and pushed me toward the back of the house. "I'm waiting. Get going."

I shuffled down the hall, dropped my pajamas on the floor, got under the shower, let tears and shower water mix, and cried Niagara Falls as quietly as I could.

We walked out to the car. The sun was too bright. I was limp and pitiful and woebegone. Diana opened the passenger door for me and I fell heavily into the seat. She exhaled the breath of the long suffering, bent down and began to move my legs into the car, like they were sticks, one at a time, picking them up like I was an invalid. I looked up at her over my sunglasses. What?

Eye contact.

Her: Gleeful. Twisted.

Me: "Get away from me."
Laughing, despite myself.

Nothing lasts forever, nothing
except Diana and me.

Diana & Shelly

I think Diana made me a "project" for our girlfriends, because after that day I was rarely alone. If I was awake, someone was almost always there. In singles and pairs, the Tuesday Girls called or came by. I made quesadillas for them. I was a bad influence. Boyfriends and husbands got their dinners late. *Too bad, so sad.* I didn't care ~ we lay in the sun and drank wine. They made me laugh. I couldn't imagine life without my girlfriends. Now that would be something to cry about.

Best Friends

Her little girl was late arriving home from school so the mother began to scold her, but stopped and asked, "Why are you so late?"

"I had to help another girl. She was in trouble," replied the daughter.

"What did you do to help her?"

Sarah & Me

Nancy, Diana, Jeanie

182

Diana, Lorrie, Janet

Diana, Lorrie, Terrie, Liz

"Oh, I sat down and helped her cry." ♥ Anon.

LOVE STINKS

Cliff was oblivious to me. He and Kimmi went to all the Christmas parties together, which I had to hear about from almost everyone I knew (it was like I had to go through everything six times, like an endurance test). When she went home to her parents for Christmas, he called and asked me to dinner. I wanted to believe it was because he missed me, but I knew it was guilt. And maybe pity. I went anyway.

With way too much water rushing under the bridge, we were strangers, hunched over, pushing holiday restaurant food around on our plates: Loss and indifference hung between us like a wall. The connection was gone, but there we were, bellied up to the bar, gluttons for punishment.

I read a book the other day. All about civilization or something. A nutty kind of a book.
Jean Harlow in DINNER AT EIGHT

NEW YEAR'S EVE 1981

Miserable. On the sofa with tea bags on my eyes.

"Love hurts, love scars, love wounds, love mars..."
The Everly Brothers

New Year 1982

NEW BEGINNINGS?

Because I fed it all the things it loved, the nightmare continued unabated. I spent my time in a wine-fueled stupor, living in the past and blaming myself. Every song on the radio pointed out how I messed up ~ "Little things I should have said and done, I just never took the time, you were always on my mind . . ." ~ and made me cry. I went to bed at night dissecting every detail: How did it all get ruined, what could I have done to make it better, all the wasted years? Two o'clock in the morning was the worst. Thank God for Pooh.

The final straw was when I ran into Cliff and "the Dim-bat" downtown. (My girlfriends were so creative with her name.) I'd stumbled out of the bookstore into the bold light of day, clutching a bag full of self-help books and almost bumped into them.

This was the first time I'd actually seen them together. Whirling before my startled eyes, a blur of blond ponytail glinting in the sun, dark glasses, giggles and big white teeth, pleated tennis skirt, frozen yogurt cups with cartoon-colored M&M'S on top. Happiness. I braced myself, horrified. Cliff actually tried to introduce me. With no time to prepare my face to blankness, feeling this big ⟶ • and praying to fall through the sidewalk, I mumbled something about being in a hurry, and got out of there. Him? I thought, Playing tennis? In the middle of a work week? Or even anytime? Fake, fake, fake. Total false advertising.

That's when I realized that in order for me to survive this breakup one of us had to leave the pond, and since it obviously wasn't going to be the big happy fish, it would have to be me.

There came a time when the risk to remain tight in the bud was more painful than the risk it took to blossom. ❦ *Anaïs Nin*

began to think of places I could go. LA, Santa Barbara, San Francisco. I weighed the pros and cons of each, but in the end I decided not to go to Jane's in Marin despite how good it sounded. None of those places were far enough away. I decided to do the thing that had always been in the back of my mind ~ and go see what it was like to live in New England.

aving been through this sort of thing with Cliff more than once in the years before we were married, I feared that no matter where I went, there was a chance he would come find me. He always did before.

This time, I would go 3,000 miles to the other side of the country. Once I got there, I would get on a boat and go seven more miles out into the Atlantic to a speck of land so small barely anyone knew it was there. If he wanted me back he was going to have to get a plane and skywrite his message of undying love in the sky over Martha's Vineyard.

I'd never forgotten the magical little island I'd seen six years earlier, with the history and the charming old houses and the wide meadows that rolled down to the sea. I remembered the leafy graveyard and how it had spoken to me. Sadly, Cliff's grandmother and her two sisters had passed away, so I wouldn't know anyone there, but it didn't matter. At least I would have some distance; maybe I could get some perspective. And no one would talk to me about Cliff.

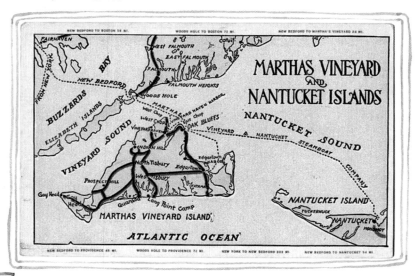

The island was small and safe; the surrounding sea provided a sort of moat. No one would be popping in. I'd always wanted to know what it would be like to have seasons, and here was my chance. I'd stay three months, rent a place to live and go from winter to spring to summer. I'd take my paints, my music, and my books. That's all I knew.

Be careful what you set your heart on, for it will surely be yours. ♥ Ralph Waldo Emerson

186

When I told Cliff I was going, the first thing he did was go to his lawyer and get a legal separation. As usual, he couldn't stand loose ends, always in a hurry. At least it wasn't an actual divorce, I was grateful for small favors. I'm sure there was some concern about his finances as they related to the laws of marriage in the state of California that I didn't understand. But it felt horrible. The impossible was becoming less so every day.

In the past, when we'd break up, I never accepted money from Cliff. I had too much distain for all that he was. It was my way of punishing him. Take that! I just moved in with a girlfriend and got a job. I'm sure there was an element of guilt, not to mention an eye toward an eventual divorce settlement, when he put money into my account so I could go. Or maybe he was just making it easy. I had no doubt that he wanted me gone as much as I wanted to get away. That way he could go about his business without accidentally running into me, or my recriminations, or bear any sort of witness to my broken heart. I don't think he meant to hurt me. I don't think he did any of it on purpose. It may not have been him at all. It might have been me.

Crowd cheers as jury clears redhead of driving car over refrigerator repairman.
Roxie Hart, newspaper headline

The Tuesday Girls had a going-away party for me at Diana's. We drank margaritas and they tried to talk me out of going, but we all could see the problem. Besides, they had their own lives to live: jobs, husbands, boyfriends, and children to look after and worry about. I was like an unmanned hot air balloon. I bought a plane ticket to Boston and started packing.

Once I made my mind up to go, I couldn't wait to get out of there.

It was early March 1982, still cold on the East Coast. I packed my suitcases with every warm piece of clothing I owned. I filled cardboard boxes with things to make a home out of a rental house: a set of towels and sheets, my grandma's nap blanket, photos and magnets for whatever fridge I'd be using, a couple of cookbooks, my favorite mug, extra sweaters, things I thought I would need during a three-month stay. I mailed the boxes to myself in care of general delivery on the Island. Five boxes full of home. But, because I didn't know where I would end up, I couldn't take the one thing that would have given me the most comfort (other than my girlfriends), and that was Pooh.

"Shelly, I know you're busy but while I'm gone, please don't forget about Pooh. Remember, she doesn't have hands; she can't open the door herself, she can't feed herself, and she's been through a lot. Get her in before dark and make sure you leave the bed-room door open so she can sleep with you."

I was cradling Pooh in my arms, and she was struggling to get away. Her paw pushed on my chin, but she was purring and I held tight and put my finger on her pink-eraser nose.

188

Shelly looked up from the table where she was writing a letter. "I promise, I'll take good care of her. I love her just as much as you do. She's going to be fine. Don't worry."

I told Shelly the rent was paid through June. I gave her money for cat food, wrote down the phone number for the vet, and asked her to forward my bills to the Island. I said when I got some-where I'd call with a phone number so she'd be able to reach me.

I could see the drama in my decision to go so far away, but it was only for three months and I desperately needed to give the whole thing a rest. Maybe when I get back to California in June, I thought, maybe something will have changed. Maybe that girl will have crawled back into the woodwork where she came from. Maybe I'll know what to do next.

In the meantime, I wrote in my diary, while I'm away, maybe I'll do what Jane suggested and try to write a cookbook. I hadn't painted anything for over six months, not since I moved out of my house. I didn't know if I still could.

It's overdoing the thing to die of love.
French Proverb

A VACATION BY THE SEA IN STORE
FOR YOU SOON.

DO YOU REMEMBER I'M ON A PLANE?

I had fallen asleep from pure exhaustion, drifting in dreams and memories when the stewardess shook me awake to ask if I was okay. I felt tears on my face. It took a moment to get my bearings, before I realized where I was: On a night flight to Boston because I was running away from home ~ and now I'd been discovered by a stranger to be crying in my sleep. I said, yes, yes, I'm fine, and asked for another blanket and looked around hoping I hadn't made any strange noises. There were just a few pinpoints of light here and there in the dark cabin but everyone seemed to be asleep. I looked at my watch and figured (scientifically, because that was my nature) we were probably over Indiana. I tried not to think about how many feet 30,000 really was, and went back to sleep.

CLOSURE

PAINTING THE BUNNY

The Constitution only guarantees the American people the right to pursue happiness. You have to catch it yourself.
♥ Benjamin Franklin

Chapter Twelve
SMALLVILLE
USA

Life itself is the most wonderful fairy tale of all.
♥ Hans Christian Andersen

There was a good reason I grew up to expect a fairy tale life and fall apart when the fairy tale turned out to be a total figment of my imagination. My mom was 17 when I was born (only five years past 12) and my dad was 23. I was raised by children ～ or at least one child and one young adult.

Everything I understood about life came from old movies, old music, and library books. Since no one told me life *wouldn't* be a fairy tale, I pretty much had my heart set on it. I'm sure my parents thought their life was a fairy tale, too.

My brothers and sisters and I were blessed with our mother's incredibly happy disposition: She sang us awake in the morning, she sang in the car, and she sang all day while she worked around the house. Along with the Shirley Temple movies she taught me to love, my mom's singing was the soundtrack of my childhood.

My M♥m, the original Fairy Tale Girl.♥

"Are you the reason my happy heart sings?
But definitely..." ♥ Shirley Temple

191

y dad looked like Frank Sinatra in 1945 when he and my mother met. Blue-eyed with black curly hair, John Patrick Stewart Jr. was just home from World War II and Iwo Jima, happy to be alive, and wearing his white sailor uniform the afternoon he spied 15-year-old Patricia Louise Smith at a dance in a hotel in Long Beach, California. She'd gone there with a girlfriend to hear the big band music (an event not sanctioned by her mother).

My mom felt comfortable with my dad from the start; he had that same take-charge attitude as her dad, my grandfather, Willard Smith. In my mother, my father saw a mystery wrapped in an enigma that he wished to investigate for a lifetime.

uring their yearlong courtship, they discovered a mutual love of pork chops. So when he proposed he said, "Let's get a house and have pork chop wallpaper and pork chop furniture and a whole bunch of little pork chops running around."

In Big Bear

What starry-eyed young girl in love and believing in "happily ever after" could resist that? I was their first pork chop, with seven more following me—an even number, four girls and four boys. In our house we got a new pork chop almost every two years, and for the whole time I lived at home, it was baby powder, yellow rubber pants, plastic ducky rattles, knitted booties, and green snap-on jammies with plastic feet in them.

My parents and their friends had learned through experience that they shouldn't expect too much from life. As children they'd been humbled and shaped by the Depression, which gave them a strong work ethic; they learned early on to make do or do without and do it with a smile. In their teens, at the age when they should have been most carefree, they were plunged into four years of war. When the insecurity, sorrow and loss of that was over, every day of peace and prosperity was a gift and a blessing. They had learned the hard way what really mattered in life, and their whole generation acknowledged their good fortune by settling down, buying homes, planting gardens, and raising children.

Just before my parents were married in 1946, my dad got a job working for the phone company (and stayed there for 35 years). Two months after they married, my mom was pregnant, so they had almost a year of wedded bliss before I was born.

The Villa Riviera in Long Beach where my parents met.

*m*y mom was in labor with me for 72 hours. My theory is that during a particularly difficult contraction, a piece of her soul broke off and rolled into me, forming the nucleus of my own. There has never been a moment when I didn't feel my heart beating in time with hers. It was love at first sight.

My sleep-deprived dad was upset about his young wife and the long labor and showed his frustration by throwing a vase filled

with flowers against the wall of the waiting room and shattering it. I've always loved that story, sorry I was the cause, but I loved that my dad was the demonstrative type. They had planned to name me Candy, but by the time I finally got there, I guess they didn't think of me as a Candy anymore, so they called me Susan Anne instead.

*F*or 13 lovely months I had my parents all to myself . . . until my brother Jim arrived, then Stephen, and soon after, my brother Chuck. By that time, my parents had saved enough (along with help from the GI Bill) to buy a brand-new, four-bedroom geranium-colored house for $16,000 in the heart of the

San Fernando Valley ～ where our family would be completed
with the arrivals, over time, of four more babies, Bradley, Paula,
Mary, and Shelly.

After work and every weekend, my dad worked to improve
our house (which he called "Smallville" ～ mostly because
of the size of the inhabitants and our little life in that
house). He made bunk
beds for the boys and
enlarged the kitchen
so that we could have
a table big enough
where we could all
eat together. He poured
cement for a patio,
put a roof over it, and
built a brick barbecue
that had a fireplace
where we could roast
marshmallows.

The first seven ～ still waiting for one more

195

Sue Stewart   Feb. 7, 1957

The Story of my Life

I was born in Long Beach, in Saint Mary's
Hospital, in 1947.
Little did I know that I was to be the
oldest of six children, 4 Boys, 1 Sister.
My father worked for the Telephone Co.
before I was born and he still does.
When I was 3 years old we moved to a street
called Park ave. That was in 1950. When
we lived there we raised dogs and we
ad 2 ducks. We got eggs free. It was fun
go on a egg hunt every day.
When I first went to school I was
happy. My first school was called
Minnie Gant. I stayed there untill
second grade. Then I moved up here
in 1954.
When I was 7 years old I became
a Brownie. We have had lots of good
times together, and in June I will
Become a Girl Scout.

The End

I used to be able to get all the most important parts of my life on one page!

196

Behind the barbecue, he made a pint-sized playhouse for my little sisters, complete with window boxes. He put in brick borders for the flowerbeds and planted plums, oranges, and avocadoes in our backyard. No one taught him how to do these things. He made it all up as he went along.

My mother sewed dresses for me, shirts for my brothers, curtains for the house, and doll clothes ～ and when I was old enough, she taught me how to make my own clothes on the black Singer sewing machine that was always in the kitchen next to the baby's bassinet.

y parents took what life gave them and added to it. They created, making something from nothing every day. I don't think they ever heard of a stumbling block.

In a homemade happy life

My mom made our outfits & took tons of photos. We smiled at first, but by the time she took this one, we just wanted to go to the party.

As a child my mom loved dolls, and she always knew she would grow up and have lots of children. She said that she and I "played dolls with real babies." That's how I remember it, too. I was a toddler when I stood

next to the sofa, my hand on my bundled baby brother . . . my 18-year-old mom's voice saying, "Make sure he doesn't roll off, hold him there while I run to the bathroom, be careful." I was her little wingman from the beginning.

Mom, Uncle Bob, Uncle Dick

When we bathed our baby (whichever one it was at the time) we would close the kitchen doors and turn on the oven in the white O'Keefe and Merritt stove to make the small kitchen cozy and warm enough for the baby.

My mother set up the bassinet in the space between the stove and the refrigerator, a contraption much like an ironing board with a lid for changing the baby that opened

to a soft little rubber tub below. She poured warm water into it, tested it with her elbow; and we bathed the baby there, pink and slippery. Mom held her head while we washed her hair and rinsed it, pouring water from a measuring cup like a baptism. She squinched up her face and snorted and wiggled and laughed.

MOM'S REAL DOLLS

We blotted her dry and kissed her feet, her toes curled and drool sparkled on her lips. We powdered her and put her in a soft cotton diaper and yellow plastic pants and stuffed her fat bone-less arms through the sleeves of a tight little T-shirt and smelled her neck in that wonderful place between shoulder and ear.

We put knitted booties on her, and wrapped her tightly in a receiving blanket. We sprinkled warm formula from a glass baby bottle onto our wrists to make sure it was the right temperature.

I fed the baby while my mom put the two-year-old in a high chair and scattered Cheerios on his tray. He jumped and jiggled, pounded his tray and kicked his feet while she warmed up cans of Campbell's Chicken Noodle Soup for the other kids. There is nothing more wonderful than watching a two-year-old try to pick up a noodle from his tray.

Mary, on the bassinet, right next to the dinner table. In her spare time, Mom made the curtains with the same brown fabric she used on my polka dot dress.

When the baby was done with her bottle, I burped her and my mom came and got her and gave her a rattle and danced her over to the bassinet, singing, ♪ Mares eat oats & does eat oats & little lambs eat ivy ... ♫

So wise & right & tender a heart, it was good as genius. ♥ Margaret Oliphant

199

Under the blue skies of the San Fernando Valley where it was almost always sunny, my mom and I hung diapers together on the line in the backyard. The wind caught them; they flew up

over our heads and flapped above us like angels' wings. My mom told me what a big help I was. She called me the "*little mother*" ~ I felt important to her, needed and appreciated. We sang, "EVERYBODY'S ASKING ME, 'WHO'S THAT BUNCH of PERSON-AL-ITY?' I'M PRESENTING YOU RIGHT NOW, BABY TAKE A BOW . . ." And we both took a bow, in the wind, under the diapers, with apron strings flying. 🩷

Me & Jim washing dishes in the "throw-up pan."

Like mother like dAughter 🩷

Me with Chuckie

On my dad, in order, Paula, Brad, Chuckie, Stephen, Jim & me.

The neighborhood in the playpen

200

My parents' friends, "The Greatest Generation," and their baby boom children enjoyed family "Come as you are" breakfast parties on the weekends.

My parents rarely went out at night except to the drive-in movies, and we always went with them. They didn't drink, and swear words were verboten in our house (none of this "I wish she'd go to hell-o" when you wrote a note to your best friend in catechism class, don't even think about it). I must have come home from school with a word my mom didn't like, because she told me I could make up words; I didn't have to use the same old tired words other people used. I loved the thought of making up my own words. My first swear word was "goose-goss." Later, it was "farmer." Then "hell-o," but only once.

Sooner or later every child tells their Mom they hate her (at least we did); but every time one of us did, my mom always said the same thing, "Well, I LOVE you." She never descended to our level, no matter how much we deserved it. She was true-blue. I think sometimes we tested her just to hear her say (again) I love you.

The very feel of her hand was reassuring; it was the sort of hand that children would like to hold in the dark. ♥ Elizabeth von Arnim

Our family had its own language called "Arf and Arfy," which my mom learned as a child from the *Little Orphan Annie* comic strip in the *Sioux City Journal* in Iowa where she was born and raised. While she was still a child she taught it to my dad and later they used it to talk privately in front of us about important things like polio shots, Santa Claus, and trips to Disneyland. It didn't take long before we all caught on, and our family became bilingual. Later, I taught it to all my girlfriends. It has been very useful. Every family should have their own secret language.

The Stewart Kids

— At Knott's Berry Farm —

202

One of the best things we got from our parents was a strong sense of family pride. All for one and one for all. We moved en masse, took up a whole pew in church, and (even though we had nothing to do with it) we were very proud of being part of a family with eight children. We were "the Stewart kids," and the force was with us. All the other children in our neighborhood practically lived at our house because of our young mother who loved "little people" as she called us. Everyone was welcome, and fun was the order of the day.

Totally devoid of culture, formality, or reverence, we slept out in the backyard, played hide-and-go-seek, hunted Easter baskets, hula-hooped, roller skated, took swimming lessons, played mermaid and Marco Polo in the pool, put on shows and circuses, sold Kool-Aid, dodged giant pollywogs at the lake, fought over the Pez dispenser, complained, "Mom, Steve's lookin' at me." We traded stuff, sold stuff, broke stuff, hid stuff, and made stuff together. We played war, slap jack, crazy eights, tiddly-winks, Mr. Potato Head, and Parcheesi; we bribed, told on, teased, tortured, and took care of each other. It was loud, and it was wild; but it was a wonderful way to grow up.

Stuffed into our few years of childhood were enough stories to keep us laughing for the rest of our lives.

A tent full of babies in Sequoia Nat'l Park

Every June, as soon as school let out, in a true *masterpiece of organization*, my parents filled our station wagon with sleeping bags, pots and pans, clothes, tent, kerosene lamp, playpen, stroller, diapers, baby bottles, camp stove, and ice chest. We kids were perched on top of it all, between cereal boxes and pillows as we headed out at 4 a.m. for the eight-hour drive up to the High Sierras for a week of camping under the stars. This is how I knew my parents were crazy. Normal parents would have hired a babysitter and run away to Las Vegas.

Packed & leaving the next morning; this is a dry run, got a new baby, do we all still fit?

For the last hour of the trip to the campsite, it was one hairpin turn after another. Every year, as our overloaded station wagon slowly swayed and dipped, up and down, through steep canyons like a boat in high waves, we all threw up out every window of the car. We always felt bad for the people behind us. First thing my dad did upon arrival was stop at the gas station and hose down the car.

My parents set up camp and we spent our days luring squirrels, watching for bears, swimming in the cold mountain lake with the biggest, fattest, scariest pollywogs known to man (probably prehis-toric, the way I remember them), and riding mules on hot dusty trails through giant, ancient Sequoia trees. It was my first taste of the silence and beauty and grandeur of nature. We roasted marshmallows and weenies over an open fire and watched the sparks go up into the black sky thick with stars and Sputniks while our dad told us scary ghost stories.

In the chilly morning, my dad got up first and made a fire. Pretty soon my mom put on coffee and started frying bacon. My memories are filled with the evocative aromas of the musty tent, damp Hopalong Cassidy flannel-lined sleeping bags, break-fast sizzling in an iron pan, coffee, hot dirt mixed with pine needles, and wood smoke. I helped my mom wash dishes in a sudsy bucket filled with warm water we heated over the campfire in the shady, dappled sunlight shining through the pines. Deep breath of pine, ahhhhh.

205

The moon was high & full & all the world was purple shadow & silver.
Frances Hodgson Burnett ♥ The Secret Garden

Daisy & Betty (the ducks), Cindy (the dog), me, Stephen & Jim

Jim helping Dad & me 'helping' Jim

206

Chapter Thirteen
The Sweet Life

The reason I should never fly. I don't like to be off the ground. Trying not to strangle Stephen & hoping the baby will save me.

By the time all the children were born, my mom's busy life included, for starters, the preparation of 30 meals a day. There was always something in the oven, and except for the occasional liver night, our house smelled wonderful.

My mother had an interesting relationship to food: she didn't refer to it by its actual name, such as potatoes, chicken, and lettuce. She looked at food scientifically, as fuel to build strong bones and teeth; she called it "starch, protein, & roughage." Ice cream was "calcium."

"Honey, you're not eating enough roughage," she would say, pointing to what the rest of the world called salad.

Our dinners were made up of two parts roughage, one part protein, one part starch, and for dessert, we had ice cream,

♪ GOSH OH GEE AIN'T WE GOT FUN...SWALLOWING ANIMALS ONE-BY-ONE ♪

207

which she considered practically a health food. Never any soft drinks, they were too expensive, a complete waste of money; we all drank milk for dinner, including my parents, and everyone cleaned their plates because of the starving children in foreign countries.

OCT · 55

me   Jim

Stephen   Chuckie

Her children rise up & call her blessed.
♥ *Proverbs 31:28*

No one could make a better bowl-licking potato salad or fall-off-the-bone spareribs than my mom; her grilled cheese sandwiches were ambrosia (her secret? Mashing down the sandwiches with a spatula as they cook). Our photo albums are filled with her birthday cakes, two or three layers, frosted in mint green or pink, speckled with crushed peppermint or candy sprinkles. She baked "lucky dimes" inside for us to find at birthday parties (not a problem, choking hazards had not been invented yet), and everyone at the party got their own cupcake with a candle to make a wish on. Because of us, she would make any recipe that featured miniature marshmallows, chocolate chips, or Jell-O ~ or potato chips: ~ which were mashed into our bologna sandwiches and crushed on top of our tuna casseroles. She even made cookies with potato chips.

By the time I was 10, while the baby napped and my mom folded diapers at the kitchen table, I was whirling batter in the Mixmaster, wearing one of my great-grandma's embroidered flour sacks tied up under my arms as an apron. My mom taught me how to sift flour, cream butter and sugar, melt chocolate without burning it, and break eggs. As Mother's little helper and future-mother-in- training, I made brownies and peanut butter cookies for school lunches and passed out beaters and bowls to my brothers and sisters

to lick. I frosted cup-cakes, stirred chocolate syrup into milk, made cinnamon toast, tied bibs on babies with Cheerios stuck to their cheeks, stirred together sticky masses of marshmallows and Rice Krispies, arranged fish sticks and tater tots on a baking sheet. Helping my mother was like playing house ~ I loved it.

·MOM'S·
POTATO CHIP
C O O K I E S
350° MAKES 3 DOZEN
1 c. BUTTER,
  SOFTENED
1/2 c. SUGAR
1 TSP. VANILLA
2 c. FLOUR
1/2 c. CHOPPED
  PECANS
1 1/2 c. CRUSHED
  POTATO CHIPS
(W/ ROLLING PIN)

PREHEAT OVEN TO 350°. CREAM BUTTER & SUGAR UNTIL LEMON-COLORED. STIR IN ALL OTHER INGRED. & COMBINE WELL. ROLL INTO SMALL BALLS & PLACE ON LIGHTLY BUTTERED COOKIE SHEET. FLATTEN BALLS WITH BOTTOM OF GLASS (DIP IN POWDERED SUGAR TO PREVENT STICKING). BAKE 15 MIN. UNTIL LIGHT BROWN. ♥ PUT IN TUPPERWARE; TAKE CAMPING. DELICIOUS WITH GRAPE KOOL-AID. ·

earned my Girl Scout cooking badge by making a special main dish for my family: I slit hotdogs down the middle, stuffed them with Velveeta cheese, wrapped them with bacon strips, and broiled them to bubbling, sizzling perfection. My brothers said they liked them as much as fried bologna, which was a HUGE compliment. I was so proud, I took a picture of them.

I was almost 11 when I arranged this photo of gracious living, with the vase of plastic flowers and the open cookbook. Like this recipe came out of a cookbook! I think I was just beginning to catch on to the decorative possibilities with food, but didn't yet understand that this might not be the food to do it with.

It's a wonder we didn't have teeny little heart attacks.

The Bomb Shelter
Or A day in the life of Smallville

In case you are too adorably young to remember, in the 1950s there was a cold war between America and Russia and lots of anxiety in our country about the threat of nuclear annihilation. In 1957, when I was 10, President Eisenhower's administration began to actively promote the building of backyard bomb shelters.

Like everything my dad did, his bomb shelter was a masterpiece of design and efficiency. He drew us a picture of how the bunk beds would fold against the wall during the day; where we'd keep our

My dad made this patio & cover, including totem pole. The bomb shelter was behind it.

sleeping bags and pillows; the drawer for our games; where Nipper, our dog, would sleep; the shelves for peanut butter and tuna. Stephen, who was seven, piped up, "Where will we keep the throw-up pan?" We laughed. Fascinating question! It was exciting. It was cozy. We thought life in the bomb-shelter would be like camping.

Every day my dad came home from work, changed out of his suit, grabbed his shovel, and went out behind the barbecue to dig the hole. It was a lot of work; it was a really big hole. The dirt pile on the driveway had grown so high, he had to run at it with the wheelbarrow in order to dump the dirt over the top. Sweat poured down his face and neck.

While digging, he had plenty of time to think; and soon, for more reasons than one, he began to question this solution to the problem of the atomic bomb.

Our neighborhood was filled with big families just like ours. No one could miss the pile of dirt in our yard; everyone knew my dad was building a bomb shelter.

A few of our neighbors at the
playhouse behind the BBQ
(next to the bomb shelter)

They all came by to check it out, adults and kids with bikes, standing at the edge of the hole, looking down, asking questions and making jokes about digging to China.

"Dad?" I asked one night at the dinner table, "If the bomb drops, I told Karen she could come into the shelter with us, OK?"

I was sure my best friend would be welcomed with open arms. Since there were no girls in the family near my age, I almost always got to take a friend with me when we went places.

"Yeah," my brother Jim chimed in, "I told Kevin he could come, too."

"I don't think so," my dad said, from his spot at the head of the table, buttering a slice of bread. "There's not going to be room. Only one bed for each of us."

This was the first time it occurred to me to think about the actual size of the hole. Six feet by 10 and 12 feet deep. At the time, we were a family of eight plus Nipper.

More neighbors, Betsy Bennett,
Karen's sister, is in front.

"But, Jack," my mother said thoughtfully from the other end of the table, "what if Karen or Kevin are here when it happens? Won't we just take them with us?"

Nipper

I was nodding at my mom. She made perfect sense. I looked back to my dad.

"I've been thinking about that," said my dad. "What about Karen's sisters?" Karen had four sisters and lived one house over from us. "What if they want in? What about the Burrows and the Pfennings? Are we supposed to let them in, too? What are we going to do if the whole neighborhood comes down here and tries to get in with us? It could be a riot. We'd have to defend the bomb shelter ~ we'd probably have to shoot them."

Top three girls on left are Karen & two sisters, Kathy and Joanie. Judy Burrows is standing next to me

WHAT?

The people at the table old enough to get his meaning gasped in alarm and recognition of some sort of weird truth. Jim quit feeding Nipper under the table; Stephen stopped gnawing on his spare rib; almost on cue Paula started crying in her high chair. We all looked at Dad. Our dad went deer hunting every year. We knew he had guns.

SHOOT Karen and the Burrows? My head whipped to the other end of the table, to my mother who looked up while putting a scoop of mashed potatoes on Chuckie's plate. Her gaze landed on my dad with an audible *thunk*. Shaking her head, she said what she always did when my dad said something she didn't want us to hear, "Jaaaaaaaack?" Never has there been more meaning expressed in just one word. We knew it, and he knew it.

Just home from church, the people Dad was trying to protect ♡

In Arf and Arfy she said, "Darfont tarfalk arfabarfout tharfis arfin frarfont arfov tharfa karfids" (Don't talk about this in front of the kids).

I was already fluent in Arf and Arfy, and hearing this didn't help.

My dad shook his head in an *It's not my fault* way and piled some roughage on his plate.

"Pat," he said, "do you think we are putting the entire neighborhood in there? *Think* for a moment. Look at that hole!"

We do not discuss the members of our family to their faces. ♡ *Ivy Compton-Burnett*

Chastising him with a sharp look that bounced off his head like a Frisbee, my mom glanced around the table at the questioning, disbelieving (Is this a joke? Our dad was always making jokes), innocent faces staring back at her, but it was too late.

There was a slow, intense realization that even though our mom was now fake laughing, there was a distinct possibility that we would be shooting the neighbors to protect the hole we were going to be living in because the air outside was supposedly poison, and our house was going to be gone. This was not like camping.

My eyes filled with tears. Up until then my biggest fear was that I might accidentally take the powdery stuff off a butterfly's wings.

"Are there going to be dead people all over the ground when we come out?" I asked in a quivering voice, having experienced the ultimate appetite suppressant.
Jim, with worried eyes, sucking the neck of his T-shirt, looked at my mom and waited.

Please don't make us shoot the neighbors...

"No. Don't think about it," my mother said firmly, head shaking. "This isn't dinnertime conversation. No one is shooting anyone around here." She turned to me, "Eat your dinner, honey, use your napkin, you haven't had your starch. Jim? Your roughage? Stop sucking your T-shirt and eat."

Like a balloon whizzing around the room, losing air with that motorboat noise it makes until it falls flat on the floor with a thwap, that's the way our family enthusiasm went out of the bomb shelter project. It was over. If we were going to have to shoot the neighbors, we didn't want a bomb shelter. We did what our mother told us and tried not to think about it. If there was a cartoon of us, it would be eight ostriches with their heads comfortably buried in the sand. What bomb?

My dad seemed good with it and went to the living room to eat his ice cream. He stretched out on the floor in front of the TV, turned on Red Skelton, and rolled with laughter at Clem Kadiddlehopper until tears streamed from his eyes. That made us feel better. When our dad laughed like that, which he did all the time, everything was right with the world.

Isn't it interesting that all that worry and fear was for nothing?

And don't YOU worry. Nothing was ever wasted at our house. The big hole in our backyard went to good use. My dad buried our broken cribs, strollers, camping equipment, and old yard furniture there (our own little time capsule). When it was filled and he could stuff nothing more into it, he built a sand box over it. And it isn't as if he had nothing left to do. He could go dig the swimming pool (where the whole neighborhood would be welcome). But that's another story; talk about dirt piles! This book isn't long enough for the imagination and energy of my father.

I'm not one of those complicated mixed-up cats. I just go day-to-day taking what comes.
Frank Sinatra ~ good kitty

BEFORE & AFTER

We were so excited to move to our new house.

He was always inviting new people to come live with us.

Dad could charm a dog off a meat wagon.
Rita Mae Brown

He laid the bricks, planted the lawn, made the fence & carved the signs.

A loving heart·

M♥THERHOOD 101

My Mom's Best Advice:

Where there's a will there's a way.

Organization is the key to success

THINK BEFORE YOU SPEAK

Singing makes everything BETTER

·is the truest wisdom.·
Charles Dickens

If you don't stop your face will freeze like that.

Money doesn't grow on trees

ALWAYS WEAR CLEAN UNDERWEAR IN CASE YOU'RE IN AN ACCIDENT

USING YOUR HEAD
PATRICIA STEWART

You know the *Difference* between RIGHT & WRONG

Be a lady

The smallest of things can make you feel like something is special about today.

Don't forget your camera.

CHAPTER FOURTEEN
Faith & Pixie Dust
Making ends meet . . .

My mom lived by the old adage: "Eat it up; use it up; make do; or do without." She could stretch a dollar around the block, and she wasted nothing. For example, she put her daily to-do lists on one piece of 8 1/2" x 11" lined school paper, which she folded to give herself six rectangular shapes; each for a list, as needed, refolding as the days went by. "Why waste paper?" she said. That, in a nutshell, is why we had so much.

That and this: To make ends meet for our growing family, my dad sometimes took extra jobs, working at a hardware store on the weekend or stuffing newspapers at night. Our family lived paycheck to paycheck. There was enough to pay the bills; but the only savings account was the Christmas Club, which didn't always cover Santa's extravagant visits. None of my

mother's friends worked outside of the house, but sometimes after the holidays, my mom would work nights for a few weeks as a waitress. We all hated it. When she was away at dinnertime, the light went out of the room. She made us dinner before

219

she went to work, but it wasn't the food we wanted; it was her. We were probably the last generation to be greeted after school every day by a mom with a cookie; it was a very great blessing for which I'm forever *grateful*.

Finding JOY in everyday things... ♥

She never seemed to worry, just tied a ribbon in her hair and sang, "Would you like to swing on a star, carry moonbeams home in a jar . . . ," got down on the kitchen floor, threw out the jacks, and started tossing the ball into the air . . . she required no thanks.

Contentment is natural wealth.
♥ Socrates

I don't think my parents ever knew what they did for us. They were too busy doing what needed to be done. Every year we got new back-to-school shoes, but my mother hardly ever got new shoes and she never complained. As far as she was concerned, we were rich as Rockefeller; I never heard her wish for more. She made us feel like we had everything, and we thought so, too. I started babysitting out of the house when I was 10, had my first "real" job wrapping donuts for a neighborhood market at 14. My brothers all had paper routes; we took back bottles, sold Christmas cards and cookies, and learned to be enterprising.

In those days the supermarkets had rules. When certain things went on sale, such as sugar, it would be "one to a customer."

This irritated my mother to no end, so that's when all her children became "customers." Off we went in the station wagon to the market to buy sugar. There we were, each of us in a different line, all looking alike, dark-haired with freckled noses, three or four feet tall, wearing jeans and T-shirts and no shoes in the summer; the boys had matching butch haircuts (my dad cut their hair), and I was in braids.

Each of us clutched a single dollar bill and struggled to carry a five-pound bag of sugar. We darted our eyes at each other, giggled and looked away quickly, pretending we didn't know each other ~ proud, anti-establishment child outlaws. Very tricky. I'm sure no one figured us out.

The American Dream

Nowadays it seems impossible That anyone could raise eight children on a one-person salary, but my parents didn't do it alone. After the war, our government & all Americans set themselves to rebuilding the country. College educations for returning soldiers & loans for new homes like ours were subsidized by the GI Bill. The government built new schools, like the ones we went to, as fast as they could; unions were strong; workers were protected. Everyone paid taxes, but corporations contributed 50% of their profit & the highest wage earners paid 90%. In order to make the whole country strong, most of the very rich managed to struggle through life with a mere 10 million in the bank. They were patriots & did not abandon us to take their money, their businesses, & their jobs away to foreign lands. There was dignity in the middle class; we had houses & jobs. Homelessness was rare. A parent could afford to stay home & take care of the kids, & everyone could go to Disneyland. It was really nice. The lovely American Dream.

My mother ironed every night while we did dishes or homework or watched TV. It was part of her understanding of self-respect, to make the world a better place by having clean, ironed children.

Perfectly ironed children.

My sister Mary on a mule, wearing a starched, ironed dress. (Ben, the mule man, came through the neighborhood like the ice cream man, giving rides to children.) She rode & I walked along beside her.

I can iron tiny starched puffed sleeves on a baby's dress. Believe me, it's an art. My mom taught me how to do this around the same time she taught me to knit washcloths, and embroider dish towels and pillowcases ~ like my grandmother taught her.

THE STEWART HOUSE

The last surviving dish towel I made for my mom as a child.

THE ART OF THE
Baby Sleeve

Lay the damp sleeve with the armhole in the center. Turn it over, push the point of the iron from the outside of the sleeve toward the gathers. It leaves a crease in the sleeve which makes it look very perky.

It was important to my mom that things were clean and organized (or at least somewhat bearable) for my dad when he got home from his hard day at the office. She'd rush around clearing up the clutter, change the baby, tie on a clean apron, apply fresh lipstick, and mash the potatoes. Dinner was always ready at six o'clock sharp. We kids ran free all day, on our bikes, playing in the street, to our friends, to the library, to the Piggly Wiggly to get a Coke, but everyone knew to be home by six (or else).

If I was to rate the division of power in our family, it would go something like this: one vote for all the children together (which could disappear in an instant), five votes for my mom (except during the day when my dad wasn't home, then she got seven), and 10 for my dad, who was always the final authority on everything.

In our house it was my mom's job, and mine, too, to care for babies, put clean sheets on the beds, grocery shop, prepare food, sterilize bottles, and do laundry. The boys (and my dad) took care of the yard, worked on the car, and handled everything that required a tool from the garage. There was a strict division of housework by gender. If there were going to be flowers in a vase, it would not be the boys who would do it. And my mother and I did not take out trash.

Happy Mother's Day. I Love you.

GIRL SCOUT · CHILD CARE BADGE

"Here, Jim," my mother said to my eight-year-old brother, "sit down here and feed the baby for me."

"I'm goin' outside."

"No, you're sitting right here so I can peel the potatoes. You might as well learn how to do it; you'll be getting married someday and having a baby of your own."

Revulsion crossed his face.

"I'm never getting married."

"I think you will, honey. Most men do."

Jim, Shelly & Mary

Jim couldn't roll his eyes (just like he couldn't skip or say his r's yet), so he looked up and to the right and slowly rolled his head around his fixed eyes. He'd made himself clear.

OUR SONG

BEST SUNG IN DAVY CROCKETT COONSKIN HAT

"...Oh, they ran through the briars & they ran through the brambles & they ran through the bushes where the rabbits couldn't go..."

JIMMY DRIFTWOOD

rowing up as the oldest and in such close proximity to my brothers, I took it for granted that my opinion carried at least the same weight as theirs ~ more sometimes, because I was the unofficial safety monitor ~ in charge of shoes, socks, jackets, when to cross the street, and what should or should not be put into mouths. No one warned

Chuckie, me, & our cousin, Coral

me against this kind of thinking except for the occasional, "You're not the boss of me."

Men on bike. (Don't try this at home.)

We were so alike, me and my brothers, two arms, two legs, 10 fingers; we ate, we ran; we rode our bikes, we laughed and cried; and we all did it alike. Other than their puzzling attraction to near-death experiences, I could not tell the differ-

We all loved to eat olives off our fingers.

ence between them and me. I could do yo-yos, they could do yo-yos; I could Walk the Dog and Go around the World, and so could they. I rode bikes, they rode bikes; we all played hide-and-go-seek with equal expertise.

Jim's 8th Birthday, Stephen doing favorite dance, me (back right), serving.

225

I could play jacks and a highly competitive game of hopscotch (which, let's face it, they couldn't have won even if they wanted to). And that is where we parted company. They would not be caught dead playing "girl" games. The worst thing you could say to my brothers is, "You run like a girl." They would roll into a ball like a pill-bug at the thought of it. I never understood what was wrong with that. I ran like a girl.

"Alas, Mother, I have knocked my brother's head off!" And she wept & & wept & could not be comforted.
~Brothers Grimm

I would watch them slap, smack, and pretend to poke each other's eyes out, saying "soitenly" a hundred times like their heroes, the Three Stooges, and feel superior. In my whole life, I would never once do that. I was sure I couldn't possibly be MORE of an idiot than they were. Maybe about the same. But definitely not worse.

Something you don't see much anymore, boys with their mom's nylon stockings over their heads.

When they jumped off the garage roof, using heavy canvas as a parachute, thereby breaking their legs and arms; or did belly flops in the pool on purpose; or put snakes on the kitchen table and sharpened ice cream sticks into little prison knives by rubbing

Chuckie and Bradley

them on the driveway, I would look at my mom with a question in my eyes, and she would answer with a shrug of her shoulders. We didn't know why they did these things. It was a mystery. On the way to the emergency room, she would sigh and say, "Boys will be boys." They punched each other, laughed, and said, "Oh, Pancho. Oh, Cisco."

The highlight of my childhood was making my brother laugh so hard that food came out his nose. ♥ Garrison Keillor

On the nights the boys played Pop Warner football, my dad gave them T-bone steaks for

Cute Cisco and Adorable Pancho were football stars in highschool.

dinner so that they would be animals on the field. The rest of us didn't need to be animals, so we had our normal macaroni and cheese or Spanish rice.

Let me not be sad because I am born a woman In this world; many saints suffer in this way. ♥ Janabai (c.1340)

The sainted ones, wearing fabulous leopard: me, Mary, Shelly, Paula

227

Until I was 12, I always shared a room with the youngest baby. But after that, my parents had a room, my four brothers were in two sets of bunk beds in another room, and the little girls shared a third bedroom.

Which meant that, in the wild pandemonium of our household, at 12 years old, I had my own room, with a door I could close ~ a room I could decorate just like the "teenage" bedrooms I saw in my Seventeen magazines, where I could while away dreamy hours gazing at cracks in the ceiling, reading, or writing in my diary, with the windows wide open, listening

to the ice-cream truck jingle by, while sunlight and shadows played across my walls. At night I could listen to my transistor radio, look up from my pillow out the window and see the stars, ponder the secrets of the universe, and ask myself the important questions, like . . .

Which would you rather be if you had the choice ~ divinely beautiful, dazzingly clever, or angelically good?

♡ L. M. Montgomery

LIBRARY DAYS

Little Red Riding Hood was my first love. I felt that if I could have married Little Red Riding Hood, I should have known happiness.

CHARLES DICKENS

Once I discovered the joys of reading, I almost lived at the public library, just two blocks over from our house. I was drawn to fairy tales by the Brothers Grimm and Hans Christian

Andersen, but especially the old books with colors for titles: The Green Fairy Book, The Lilac Fairy Book, The Crimson Fairy Book. There were a dozen of these books, in all colors, in the Reseda Public Library, published between 1889 and 1910, filled with tales and folklore from all over the world: stories collected (and probably rescued from obscurity) by a Scots poet named Andrew Lang. I read them all.

So labour at your Alphabet,
For by that learning
Shall you get
To lands where Fairies may
be met. ♥ Andrew Lang

These were not your regular fairy tales. These were magical, sometimes scary, stories where trolls and elves slept in hollow trees and "frolicsome fairy winds" could "carry a baby away like a dandelion seed." Fantastical stories filled with mystery and adventure where

229

setbacks were unavoidable; but if you kept your head and carried on, anything was possible. My favorites were stories that began with the thrilling words, "Once upon a time" ~ and ended, "And they lived happily ever after." Sigh, deep breath, close eyes, hug book to chest, ahhhhh.

The loveliest tinkle as of golden bells answered him. It is fairy language. You ordinary children can never hear it, but if you were to hear it, you would know that you had heard it once before. ♥ J.M. Barrie

The library was quiet & air-conditioned & it smelled wonderful. It was my summer haven.

MAKE A DREAMS IMAGINATION
Wish CREATIVITY DARING TRUE LOVE
magic DEEDS
SPELLS ADVENTURE
THE WORLD

HAPPILY EVER AFTER
RESOURCEFULNESS INSPIRATION
enchantment Once Upon a Time INVENTION

You hail from dreamland dragon-fly?
A stranger hither? So am I.
A. Mary F. Robinson

It was easy to believe that some of these fairy stories about giants and elves and talking trees could be true. We knew kids weren't writing them; it was adults who were telling us there were fairies and magic. The very same people who wrote our schoolbooks. Around this time, I started closing my closet door before I got into bed, just in case there were wolves.

All-of-a-kind Family SYDNEY TAYLOR

Everything was romantic in my imagination. The woods were peopled by the mysterious good folk. ♥ Beatrix Potter

In the summer, once school was out, I walked to the library barefoot and came home with my arms overflowing with romance, fantasy, adventure, history, and inspiration, with books like *All of a Kind Family*, *Anne of Green Gables*, and *Little Women* ～ and when I was older, *The Diary of Anne Frank*, *Seventeenth Summer*, *To Kill a Mockingbird*, and *Marjorie Morningstar*. I was inspired by all of them, but reading *Pollyanna* when I was nine years old changed my short little life. That's where I learned about "The Glad Game," which said that no matter what the situation, a person could always find something to be happy about if they tried. Which meant I could choose how to think! That's a lot of power for a nine-year-old ～ like taking the lid off a jar of butterflies.

One gift the fairies gave me: (three, they commonly bestowed of yore:) the love of books, the golden key, That opens the enchanted door. ♥ Andrew Lang

231

When I finished reading Gone with the Wind, I was such a mess from sobbing my heart out that I couldn't go to the dinner table. I was 15 and completely beside myself. In fact, for years Gone with the Wind is where I would go whenever I felt like a good cry. I would start at the part where Melly Wilkes was dying and sob all the way to the end. I'd close the book and lie there in the quiet, thinking how blind Scarlett had been ~ glad she was going home to Tara to get her strength back. Rhett would come get her ~ I knew he would, he'd loved her for so long . . . but the question was, how could any

that be your cross. Well, the cross was heavier now. It was bad enough that she had tried by every art to take Ashley from her. But now it was worse that Melanie, who had trusted her blindly through life, was laying the same love and trust on her in death. No, she could not speak. She could not even say again: "Make an effort to live." She must let her go easily, without a struggle, without tears, without sorrow.

The door opened slightly and Dr. Meade stood on the threshold, beckoning imperiously. Scarlett bent over the bed, choking back her tears and taking Melanie's hand, laid it against her cheek.

"Good night," she said, and her voice was steadier than she thought it possibly could be.

"Promise me—" came the whisper, very softly now.

"Anything, darling."

"Captain Butler—be kind to him. He—loves you so."

GONE WITH the WIND

MARGARET MITCHELL

of us live without Melly? I did not know. Tears ran down my cheeks and into my ears . . . sigh, deep breath, close eyes, hug book to chest, ahhhhhh.

Give me a moment, because I like to cry for joy. It's so delicious, to cry for joy. ♥ Charles Dickens

From what I could see, the world was on the side of the good and the true. We were not alone. There was help out there; for one thing, we had Superman fighting for truth, justice, and the

American way. Walt Disney provided the magic. Every Sunday night we sang along with "When you wish upon a star . . ." Our influences were hopeful ∼ fairies, not vampires.

ALL THE WORLD IS MADE of FAITH & PIXIE DUST.
♥ J.M. Barrie

Therefore: I believed in Santa Claus until I was 12. I think my mom helped that along in order to protect the little kids from my big mouth, but it was easy to see that believing was better than not believing. So when my mom finally forced herself to tell me (alone one night, driving in the car), I sat there with tears in my eyes. Losing Santa, Rudolph, and Mrs. Claus was terrible enough, but there was collateral damage ∼ the Easter Bunny went, too, and my personal favorite, the Tooth Fairy. Good friends, hope for the world, all gone.

Not believe in Santa Claus?
You might as well not
believe in fairies!
♥ Frank Church

It didn't stop me from believing, because I saw a difference in what I would now call "corporate" fairies and the real thing ∼ elves, pixies, brownies, and real fairies, all of which are much trickier and smarter than adults, which is why they survived. Faith is not a thing to mess with; in order for it to endure, certain realities must be ignored.

"Stop the kyllynge!" In the time of Henry III of England, a law was made which prescribed the death penalty for the "Kyllynge, wowndynge, or mamynge," of fairies ～ and it was universally respected. ♥Ambrose Bierce

My parents gave me my first diary when I was ten. It was red, it had a lock, and I was thrilled.

"Here's where you put the date," said my mom, leaning close to me, her hair smelling like Breck shampoo. "Every day you write down all   the good things that happen to you, where you go, who you meet ～ all your secrets go here." Secrets! I thought, Eureka!

"See these blank pages? They're for your future. You won't know what to write on them until you get there. When it's finished, you'll have a book of your life."

Teach us delight in simple things. Rudyard Kipling

The idea of my "whole life" going into a diary appealed to me because I was born with a nostalgia gene. Most of the children's books, music, and movies I loved were popular years before I was born. My mom introduced me to old black-and-white films from her childhood, and I fell in love for a lifetime ～ starting with Shirley Temple. Fred Astaire and Ginger Rogers came next; after that, David Niven, Ingrid Bergman, Myrna Loy, Gregory-adorable-Peck, Jeanne Crain, Walter-precious-Pigeon, Audrey Hepburn, and Barbara Stanwyck. And the wonderful movies they

234

made during the glory days of Hollywood when everyone was still trying to be a good influence: Mrs. Miniver, Top Hat, The Secret Garden, The Quiet Man, Roman Holiday, Ninotchka. I would sit in the big green chair in the living room, eat my grilled cheese with my book open in my lap, watch Shall We Dance on Million Dollar Movie on TV and dream about growing up and sailing on an ocean liner in a sparkly dress. Later on, while doing dishes, my mom and I would sing, "You say to-may-to, I say to-mah-to . . ."

They say movies should be more like life. I think life should be more like the movies. ♥ Myrna Loy

Around the time I was reading Pollyanna, I asked my mom to tell me about the "olden days." I wanted an eyewitness report on the way things used to be.

My mom was a pretty 25-year-old at the time. She stared at me for a moment, made a pishing sound through her red lipstick, rolled her brown eyes, and said, "How would I know about the olden days?"

That startled me. I was sure she would know. Hadn't she been here forever? All I wanted was a firsthand account of buggy driving and buttonhooks. Maybe something about what it was like before electricity, how it was to read by candle-light, and how it felt to write with a feather pen. I didn't think that was asking too much.

235

Wee "**W**hy don't you ask your grandfather about the olden days?" she said with a laugh.

So I did. I wrote letters to all of my grandparents and asked for photos of our family in the olden days. I still have the photos they sent (most of them framed on my bathroom wall).

A bunch of people you don't know (but my mom will☺):

My grandparents, Flo and Willard, my uncles: Bob and Dick, & my mom.

My grandma, Florence Orr Smith

The flowers! So romantic for my great aunt & uncle on their 50th wedding anniversary

"*You've got mail,*" my mom called to me as I came through the door from school. "It's on your bed."

By the time I was in the fourth grade, I always had mail. My teacher told us we could write to the chambers of commerce in any city in the world and they would send us travel pamphlets and information about their countries. So I wrote them all . . . from Copenhagen to Toronto to Rio and Rome, and they sent back heavy manila envelopes ⁓ our mailman, Breezy, who had to carry them on his route, asked my mom what I was up to.

I would look at the postmark and the foreign stamps, put my nose into a just-opened envelope and imagine I was smelling the air of Paris or Salzburg. The magic of this was not something my mother could explain to the mailman. I wrote to Queen Elizabeth when I

The Orr family. My grandma is the baby. Love the bows!

Willard, 2nd from left, Iowa State Fair Pageant

was 11, and received a letter back from her Lady-in-Waiting on Windsor Castle stationery engraved with the Royal Seal. Getting this letter, with typewriter indentations on thick cream-colored paper from a true castle where an actual prince and princess lived, made me feel like a lucky person. No one else I knew had a letter from the Queen of England, or at least from her castle ∼ although it was easy to see that they could have if they wanted to.

WINDSOR CASTLE 10th April, 1958.

Dear Sue,
    I write at The Queen's command to thank you for your letter, and to explain to you that it is against Her Majesty's rule to send either her own photograph or autograph or that of her family to anyone whom she does not already know.
    When I tell you of the great many similar requests that The Queen receives, I feel sure you will understand the reason for this rule and that Her Majesty would not wish to break it for any one particular person.
    The dates of the birthdays for which you ask are:-

The Queen   - 21st April.
The Duke of Edinburgh - 10th June.
The Duke of Cornwall - 14th November.
Princess Anne   - 15th August.

        Yours sincerely,
        Kathryn Dugdale.
        Lady-in-Waiting.

AND SO IT WAS, day after day, I read my books and travel brochures in the tree my dad planted next to the porch in our back yard, wrote letters to my Grandma, made my clothes for back-to-school, played mermaid in the pool with my girlfriends, embroidered dish towels and baby bibs, gave the little kids bubble baths, slept in the backyard on summer nights, counting the stars while falling asleep, and babysat. My mom taught us how to dance with a record called "Rock around the Clock" that she bought from a television ad on American Bandstand. As Mark Twain wrote in Huckleberry Finn, "We had mighty good weather as a general thing, and nothing ever happened to us at all." And that's exactly how it was.

GIRL SCOUT

HOMEMAKER BADGE

And so it begins. GOOD-BYE, DEAREST CHILDHOOD. I loved every second of you. HELLO crazy adult world that never makes any sense. I hope you're satisfied.

I believe we all have an age for life, an age where we felt most comfortable. Mine was 12; I was strong and happy in my book-lit world, comfortable in my freckles and crooked teeth, innocent enough to think I could cut my own hair. Up until then, everything made sense. I got all A's in the sixth grade, and received commendations on my handwriting. My dad even took some-

thing I wrote to show his friends at work (a very proud moment for me). Not being 12 still feels like being in exile, like I'll be back, just not now. I hope when I go to heaven, I am 12 for eternity.

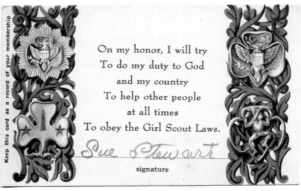

Keep this card as a record of your membership

On my honor, I will try
To do my duty to God
and my country
To help other people
at all times
To obey the Girl Scout Laws.

Sue Stewart
signature

239

Some beautiful
morning
She will just wake up,
and find it is tomorrow.
Not Today
but Tomorrow.
And then things will happen...
Wonderful things.

♥ L. M. Montgomery

You read something like this
when you're 12
and you just KNOW it's true. ♥

Chapter Fifteen
Teenage Wasteland

I'm sure there is magic in everything if only we have sense enough to get hold of it & make it do things for us. ♥ Frances Hodgson Burnett
The Secret Garden

On summer nights, after dinner, just at twilight, when we were 13, my best friend, Karen, and I would walk round and round the block, heads bent together, shoulders bumping, avoiding cracks in the sidewalk, through the neighborhood of cookie-cutter houses where we'd lived most of our lives, where dishes clattered from open windows in kitchens exactly like our own. We knew what each family had for dinner ~ smells of roast beef, fried chicken, meatloaf, and hot apple pie wafted on the breeze. Bats cracked and crowds cheered from ball games played on radios, babies cried, guys worked on their cars, sprinklers whirled, dogs wandered out to say hello, cars passed by ~ DeSotos, Dodges, Hudsons, Nashes, and Ramblers. We walked where we had once roller-skated, jump-roped, and hula-hooped, planning out loud our romantic dream of life.

Since no one was telling us, we tried to figure out how babies were made. *Is it like fish?* we wondered as we walked. Do the eggs come first and then get fertilized, or does the fertilizer come before the eggs? I don't know why we picked fish. Probably had something to do with science class. I think we were studying horseshoe crabs.

241

We hashed it over and decided the eggs must come first. Yeah, yeah, somber nodding of heads ~ that makes sense. (Because, as you can see, sense was our middle name).

We were in the seventh grade and walking across the gym field when Karen said, "I heard about this thing called French kissing."

"Really?" I said, after her long and detailed explanation.

"That's disgusting. Why do they call it French? I touched tongues with my brother when I was five and it was like licking a potato skin."

"Eeeeuw. Why'd you do that?"

"I don't know ~ we wanted to try it. We were five."

We agreed that would never happen to us and laughed ourselves silly thinking about the kind of people who would do such a yucky thing. We thought everything was funny. We walked to and from school, and barely made it home, we were laughing so hard.

In case you can't tell, we didn't get much information about sex at home in those days, none in books, none in movies (unless you counted the romantic spaghetti kiss in *Lady and the Tramp*). From the song "Town Without Pity," we learned we could be "bad" just by gazing at the stars. That didn't seem fair. There was lots of innuendo, but nothing concrete. People didn't talk about it; sex was right up there with religion and politics as something private. Girdle and bra nudity in the Sears catalog was sadly more enlightening than almost anything else. Our dads might have Playboy magazines, but they were kept in the inner sanctuary of their bedrooms, forbidden territory (on pain of death). Our popular girl singers wore Peter Pan collars and circle pins; they were goin' to the chapel and they were gonna get married. No one I knew had pierced ears, marijuana wasn't around yet (at least not at our school), and only sailors had tattoos. We stayed young a long time.

Sex wasn't the only thing our parents didn't tell us about. Early teen years were fraught with embarrassing new situations where we could "just die." From lipstick, to the hair on our legs, to Kotex, Tampax (what a nightmare, I thought I might have to call 911 dealing with that one), breasts, bras, garter belts, Noxema and boys, it was an uncharted land. When we weren't laughing hysterically, we were sobbing.

Fifteen.

No wonder I made it out into the world completely unprepared for reality.

My dad let me go on a first date to a party when I was 15 and a half ~ but only after my mother embarrassingly called and spoke to the parents (which actually weren't the parents~ as I found out later, just one of the boys who lived there pretending to be), and a more confusing, odd, and boring evening I have rarely spent.

The almost-expected stardust never appeared for even a second ~ in fact, just the opposite. As it turned out, the big excitement of the evening was an initiation for a club that was a lot like a fraternity, but for high school kids. This was in the backyard of a tract house three blocks over from where I lived. A half-dozen 15- and 16-year-old boys were lying side-by-side on their backs next to the pool. An egg was broken into the mouth of the first one and he had to drop it into the mouth of the next one and they had to keep doing this until they got the egg to the last guy on the end without breaking the yolk. I don't think they realized this was not the way to a girl's heart.

Just like home, I thought. I might as well date my brothers.

I watched about two seconds of this, and went back inside. I thought maybe I wasn't the dating type. I couldn't figure out why they invited girls to this at all, since the boys were all outside yelling while most of us were lurking self-consciously inside the house, wearing cute little party dresses, playing 45's, doing the Mashed Potato, and awkwardly slow dancing to *Theme from 'A Summer Place.'*

"Wendy," Peter Pan continued in a voice no woman has ever yet been able to resist, "Wendy, one girl is more use than 20 boys." ❥ J.M. Barrie

244

$\mathcal{B}$ut of course I was the dating type, or would be soon. I just needed to be older or maybe the boys did; but in the beginning (and many times after), dating almost always felt like an out-of-body experience. Fun sometimes, but confusing; I had no idea what I was supposed to do. Now I'm pretty sure nobody knew.

$\mathcal{I}$t's hard to go from age 12 ~ the sensible, steady world of playing with dolls, riding your bike and reading Anne of Green Gables ~ to only three years later, when you were supposed to date and slow dance to "Johnny Angel." We girls were worried sick that no boy would ever like us. Some of us did stupid things, which ensured that our worst fears would come true. It took up every waking moment, that worry about never finding a boyfriend. It made us cry.

in Tickle-Me Pink

But _we_ were the ones who smelled good, tied ribbons in our hair, practiced kissing with our pillows, knew how to make brownies, wore pink sweaters, polka-dot bikinis, and the cutest shoes. All we really had to do was stand there; sooner or later (and the later the better) someone was bound to show up. Why didn't we know that about us?

I never figured it out, and it wasn't the kind of thing I asked my parents about because it was clear they knew nothing. I was a late bloomer. I didn't have a boyfriend in high school (I hated that embarrassing question friends of my parents would ask: "Do you have a boyfriend?" It is so terrible to have to say "no" and feel yourself driving the moving van to Loser Land). I didn't go to my high school prom either. This wasn't 1946;

245

I couldn't go to my prom with my dad like Jeanne Crain did in *Cheaper by the Dozen*. In 1965, it wasn't an option.

But that didn't change my dreams, which were all about growing up, falling in love, and playing house for real. I hoped the boy part would work itself out because falling in love was a necessary dreamed-of ingredient for a romantic, rose-covered life. It seemed easy enough; it happened in all the movies. I made lists of things I needed to get for our house, including a complete grocery list. I started a hope chest in a cardboard box ～ my grandma gave me iron frying pans and

Shelly was born when I was 14½ ～ we're with our grandma.

Corningware baking dishes for Christmas, and I embroidered dish towels and baby bibs with baskets of flowers and bluebirds for my future. But the main thing in my hope chest was hope.

I got my driver's license on my 16th birthday, April 12, 1963. My mom and I bopped all the way home in the car singing with the radio, "You're sixteen, you're beautiful and you're mine . . ." Only four years past 12 and I was allowed to operate a moving vehicle. What were people thinking? But now I could be of more help to my mom with grocery shopping and getting the kids where they needed to go.

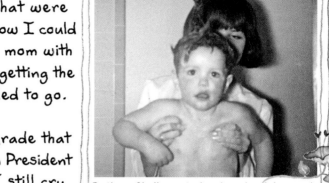

Bathing Shelly, note her hairdo. V. proud.

I was in the 11th grade that November when President Kennedy was shot. I still cry thinking about that moment, sitting in my English class staring at the brown speaker box above the blackboard, listening to the principal tell us the president of the United States was dead. My teacher cried, something I'd never seen a teacher do before. We were all sent home from school. I had babysitting jobs all weekend, and the only thing on TV was the black-and-white film of the motorcade, the Secret Service climbing on the back of the car, the First Lady carrying roses, the book depository and the grassy knoll, people sobbing ~ they played it over and over again. I couldn't even look.

It was against everything I thought life would be, so I think I mentally detached this travesty and kept it in a separate com-partment in my brain ~ in the same spot I kept World War Three. Mr. Fishbacher, my fourth-grade teacher, had told our class (in a moment of idiocy), "WWIII could break out any day," which sent me to the bathroom to cry, worried sick that my brothers (ages 3, 7, 5 and 9 at the time) would have to go fight. This horrible thought was what the special compartment in my brain was made for, and President Kennedy's assassination fit in there perfectly. I shoved it back and closed the door.

President Johnson, with his hand on the Bible, Jack Ruby shooting Lee Harvey Oswald, the crowds standing in the freezing rain at the November funeral, the drums and clip-clop of horses' hooves pulling the caisson (not a word we used, but one that became very familiar during that awful time), Jackie behind the black veil, John-John saluting the coffin ~ it all happened. It was too much to understand then, and it still is: into the compartment it all went. Every so often, I open the door to stuff in something else, and there it all is, things that no Pollyanna could touch. My own personal Pandora's box.

Life went on. You would think it would have stopped, but it didn't. Only three months after the assassination, in February 1964, the Beatles appeared on the Ed Sullivan Show; and after that, the whole world changed. People thought the sixties started in 1960, but they didn't. It was still the '50s in 1960. The '60s started in 1964.

In high school I joined the FHA (Future Homemakers of America) and was excited to follow in my mother's footsteps in my eventual career as wife and mother. For me, high school

Me, age 16, in Big Bear, barefoot & brainless in the snow. Karen, too, those are her bare feet next to me.

was three years of home economics classes, sewing and cooking, and learning secretarial skills, typing, and shorthand (in case I ever needed to help pay for Christmas for my future children). English, history, Spanish, math, and science filled out my scholastic dance card. Mostly high school was fun, seeing my friends every day, making pom-poms and learning routines for drill team, trying not to wet our pants from laughing, Friday night football games under the floodlights, slumber parties, dancing to "Runaround Sue" and "Johnny Get Angry" on spring break in Lake Arrowhead.

There was no discussion about higher education for me. My mom never needed algebra or physics to make her shopping list, so why would I? Plus (a) there was no money and (b) my parents didn't go to college. They were very young when they went off to fend for themselves. They hadn't had the time nor the experience to comprehend the value of a college education. It seemed "normal" that I would do the same as they did, marry young, have children. (c) In my neighborhood, not everyone went to college. (d) Especially not girls. (e) My brother wanted my room.

Karen and me

249

Karen graduated after I did, and when she did, she took off to Israel to live on a kibbutz for a year. After I graduated, I moved out of my parents' house and into an apartment with my other best friend, Janet. This should not have been allowed. We should have been kept locked up for at least another five years. It was a long time before we understood there was more to being grown up than just being able to reach the gas pedal. We were having way too much fun to be bothered by boring details of responsibility, the future, or that dreary thing called "maturity," which we couldn't have gotten even if we wanted it. Which we didn't.

Me and Janet

There were many good reasons for me to move out of the house, and most of them had to do with my dad: "You aren't going out in that," he said, glancing at my skirt. "Make sure you're home by 10," he said. "That Mike is a punk. Stay away from him." My mother said, "Have more ruffage, dear."

I couldn't WAIT to have my own place so that I could stay up all night, date Mike, wear short skirts, eat Taco Bell only, and have nobody tell me what to do, slow me down, or cramp my style ('cause my style was soooo happenin').

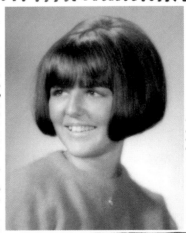

Wearing essential sweater/necklace ensemble for my senior picture

I felt bad leaving my mom alone with seven kids ranging from four to 17, but that's what she raised me to do and somehow we all seemed to think it was normal. As I kissed her good-bye, I thought I heard her whisper, "Can I come, too?"

I popped out into the world, barely six years past 12, with few skills for survival, brain barely working on one cylinder, no particular goals, no realization that I might want to have goals; in fact, What was a goal? All I had, and it wasn't nothing, was the happy gene, a true gift passed on to me from my parents ～ a belief that everything would be OK and the knowledge that if I wanted something bad enough, I could make it.

Me with our dog Nipper

Janet and I found an apartment in Encino, about two blocks off Ventura Boulevard, for $110 a month, which we could afford since we were both working. My parents gave me my bed and dresser. Janet's parents gave her hers, so our one-bedroom apartment had two double beds and two dressers along with various pieces of furniture we managed to dredge up. We were finally free and (we thought) grown up ～ something we had waited for all our lives, and we danced through our little world with joy and exuberance, because we had white patent leather go-go boots and knew all the words to every song on the radio.

Janet with her dog Pepe

251

*J*anet and I both cooked enough to get by. We fixed tea in the morning, like Janet's English mum had shown us. Janet made amazingly fluffy scrambled eggs. I cooked recipes my mom taught me, spaghetti and grilled cheese. But mostly Janet and I ate Taco Bell. Fifteen cents per taco and a little bit of heaven.

yum!

We were teenagers with our own apartment, living away from our parents for the first time. We worked nights as waitresses at Bob's Big Boy and celebrated our newfound freedom by setting peculiar hours for everything. We cleaned house at midnight, did laundry at 2 a.m., and slept 'til noon. We rolled down the windows in the car, turned up the music, sang with the radio, and drank in freedom, driving Malibu Canyon Road to Zuma Beach for fun in the sun, going to the drive-in in Janet's giant pink Dodge, practicing Arf and Arfy while waiting in line at Taco Bell. Why? Because we could. The glorious question of the young was the one we asked ourselves every morning: "What shall we do today?"

LA-DEE-DA?

LA-DEE-DA INDEED!

*D*id I mention how much fun she was? The perfect person to be 20 with. Boys loved her; they nicknamed her Natasha. I was like her pilot fish.

We always supported ourselves; we made car payments, paid our own rent, groceries, electricity, and phone bills. We split everything 50-50 and lived on our tips.

To illustrate how well we knew ourselves back then, we applied for jobs as airline stewardesses (despite our cuteness, they said no, thank God). We also tried to join the air force (it must have been the glamorous uniforms we saw in movies like *Sunday in New York* and *Boeing Boeing*); they also declined our offer ～ one of the most sensible things I ever saw the government do.

We were the type of girls who took ice-skating lessons at the Tarzana ice rink because we loved the way the little skirt flipped up when skaters went backward. We sang into our hairbrushes and dyed Janet's hair red in our kitchen sink, the same color of Ann-Margret's in *The Swinger*. We drove round and round in cul-de-sacs laughing like mad. We were not the type of girls to be entrusted with emergencies in the air or protecting the free world. If we were bored, we might even call the fire department and say, "We smell smoke," because the firemen were cute. I know (now), this was bad. Once we called the police because "We heard a noise." Cute guys in uniform: What can I say?

"On the matter of brains, I can do nothing for them," said the fairy.
♥ *Charles Perrault*

We loved the friends we made working at Bob's. It was a culture of kids; baby boomers ruled, and the whole world was our age. That's where we met Diana and became a dynamic threesome, legends in our own minds.

It was fun being a waitress, almost like a dance, hip-bumping each other in our hairnet-covered, beauty-school coiffed wiglets (de rigueur at Bob's in those days) while carrying plates of paper-wrapped Big Boy burgers up our arms like a string of popbeads. A customer could come in worn out and in a hurry, with lots of noisy, hungry kids, and I had the power to make their day. I could make them happy! I would make teeny little hot fudge sundaes in the metal cup we regularly used just for the fudge and give it to a little kid who needed cheering up (or scuttle it down my own throat like Jell-O). No two days, no two hours were the same. There were always new challenges, and it was never boring. The most important thing I learned was never to walk through the restaurant empty-handed. And always eat French fries with tartar sauce.

On busy nights, Janet and I came home with 10 dollars each in tips, which meant we didn't have to stretch a paycheck to last from payday to payday. Every day was payday. We had enough so that we could live a carefree life, which meant gas money (25 cents a gallon) to get to the beach, money for Sara Lee cheesecakes, fabric for dresses and tops, records, the cover charge at the Yum Yum Tree (where we did the Jerk and the Pony) and at Ciro's (for the Monkey and the Hully Gully), bikinis, cute bell bottoms, miniskirts, and granny glasses with pink lenses. Your basic necessities of life.

I was out of my parents' house for a year or so when it occurred to me that maybe I should try to go to college after all. So I registered at the local junior college ~ and for about a minute and a half, I actually went. Two days to be exact . . . but it was asking too much to put classes and homework into what was already an eight-hour workday, which I needed if I was going to pay the rent. You can see how that kind of discipline would be a problem for a person only seven years past 12. Where is beach time? Dance time? Diary-writing time? Boy time? Reading-books time? Sewing-new-outfit time? How did these people do it?

In the English class, I was told our final exam would be an oral book report. My hands burst into a cold sweat at the thought of it. I was happy to read the book, but I could not fathom myself standing up in front of anyone to talk about it. Not in a million years. Which meant an automatic F before I even started.

So I went back to thinking, *Why do I need this anyway?* I was just going to get married and have kids like my mom. Most of the successful people we learned about in school were men anyway; they were the ones doing everything. Men were presidents; women sewed flags. I already knew how to sew. So I quit college almost before I started. I didn't have any mentors who said, *Oh, you must go on, you will need this later.* In fact, when I told Janet I quit, she said, "Groovedelic," happy to have her girlfriend back ~ and off we went to Taco Bell to celebrate.

A society in which women are taught anything but the management of a family, the care of men, and the creation of the future generation is a society which is on its way out. ~ L. Ron Hubbard

L. Ron Hubbard would have LOVED me. Far be it from me to take down a society.

Despite Bob Dylan's premonition about the times and how they were changing, I didn't understand what it meant; I didn't even know that things COULD change. I thought the world had always been this way and always would. By the time it began to dawn on me that things were going to be different for our generation, my childhood conditioning was as much a part of me as my hands or my hair. By the time I caught on, it was difficult to change.

What is it going to be, my girl,
teaching, typing or art?
What sweet dream,
Or cloud - cuckoo scheme
Hovers over your hopeful heart?
1950 Years of Grace

Yes, you could have that totally cloud-cuckoo scheme of becoming a typist, you wild thing, you.

The future was something far off, and I didn't really have any plans for it at all. I thought it was a naturally occurring event that needed no input from me. I didn't know I had a say in it, had no idea I was already making choices. My only job (that I knew of) was to keep a sharp eye out for Prince Charming and have lots of fun until he showed up. I knew (and prayed) he was coming; and after that, it would be clear sailing, love and home and babies and happily ever after, just like in the movies.

I loved it when Johnny Mathis sang how easy he'd be to find when love came knocking at his door . . . I felt exactly the same way. So easy to find.

For Janet, Prince Charming came early. Her high-school sweetheart, Tim (who I'd known since the seventh grade), came home from Vietnam ~ he and Janet got married and moved down the coast, to Oceanside, to be near Camp Pendleton. He'd actually seen her first; their happily-ever-after had been in the works for almost as long as I'd known them.

That's when Diana, our girlfriend from work, brought her stuff from her mom's house and moved in with me.

I think it's an amazing blessing when children are aware of what they want to be when they grow up. Since she was little, Diana always knew she would be a nurse. I wished I knew, but I didn't. I even read the Yellow Pages in the phone book just to see what jobs there actually were. Nothing resonated. (No hopscotch experts were listed, nothing for homemaker, pillowcase embroiderer, or Christmas-present maker.) I didn't know then that some of us needed to grow into what we were going to be. And if you turned out to be a late bloomer, it would require patience. If you're a bit of a worrier like me, it could feel like forever; like swimming from the bottom of the sea, holding your breath the whole way, praying for some light and fresh air, and maybe even a little . . .

FAIRY

DUST

"Just living is
not enough,"
said the butterfly.
One must have
sunshine,
freedom,
and a little flower."

Hans Christian Andersen

Chapter Sixteen

SWEPT AWAY

*W*hen I used to read fairy tales, I fancied that kind of thing never happened, & now here I am in the middle of one! ♥ Lewis Carroll

*W*hile writing this book, I noticed something I never realized before: It wasn't just that I was raised by children or the baby-milk world I grew up in, or even the storybooks I loved that made me think that life would be a fairy tale. Other things happened ~ out of the blue ~ none of them huge, but odd and out of the ordinary enough to make me take notice.

*L*ike the letter from the Lady-in-Waiting at Windsor Castle when I was 11, which would seem unimportant and not especially memorable if it wasn't for the other things. I can't say these moments were caused by me or anything I was doing, because most of them showed up as a fait accompli. But they made me think I was lucky. And thinking you're lucky may be the thing that actually makes you lucky.

*F*or instance, when I was nine, I met my idol, Shirley Temple. How likely was that? Not very, since there were no movie stars in my neighborhood. But my best friend Karen's dad painted sets for NBC Studios in Burbank. One Saturday, he had to pick up something at work, and he took us with him. We were walking down an empty hallway and there, coming toward us, was Shirley Temple. Even though

259

she was all grown up, I recognized her immediately ~ she looked exactly like she did in *Bachelor and the Bobbysoxer*. I was star struck and shy and forgot to ask her how it was to work with Cary Grant, and never even tried to sing "Animal Crackers" with her. She leaned down to talk to us and could not have been nicer to two little nine-year-old girls gazing up at her in wonderment. I couldn't wait to get home and tell my mom!

A chance meeting with a childhood idol while you are still a child wouldn't be such a big deal, but then there was this . . . a story I've told many times in my life (usually shortened; this time I'll do the deluxe version):

In 1964, when we were 17 and still in high school, Karen and I bought four-dollar tickets to see the Beatles perform at the Hollywood Bowl. On the big day, we drove from our neighborhood in the San Fernando Valley to Hollywood in my parents' 1959 Chevy station wagon. (I would never let any 17-year-old of mine take a giant floater of a station wagon on the Ventura Freeway into Hollywood! Good thing I wasn't my mom.)

It was a clear, bright August evening at the famous amphitheater that was carved from a hillside in the 1920s. We could barely hear the music over the din of thousands of screaming teenagers, but that didn't matter. We could see the four fab figures from our

Me and Karen at her graduation, June 1965

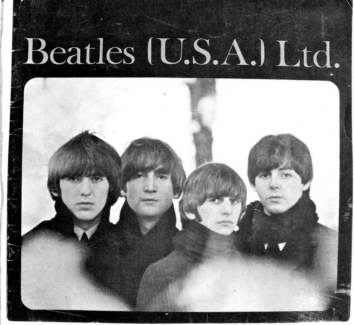

Beatles (U.S.A.) Ltd.

I still have my program from that night.

perch halfway up the side of the hill. There were actually two kinds of Beatlemaniacs: screamers and criers. Most were screamers, but we were criers. Just as frenzied as the rest, jumping up and down and clapping, singing and dancing to *She Loves You*, and *You Can't Do That*, but crying while we did it.

In the girl chatter in the restroom afterward, we heard someone say the Beatles were staying in a house in Bel Air (an exclusive West LA neighborhood filled with old movie-star mansions). So after the concert we decided to drive up Sunset Boulevard to see if we could find the house.

When we got to the entrance to Bel Air we noticed a cab parked just inside the white gates. We pulled up behind it, got out, and through his open window we begged the driver to tell us where the Beatles were staying ~ while dancing around in the street saying "*Please, please, please*" a hundred times, like only teenage girls can do. Finally, with a grin, he told us they were in a house on St. Pierre Road, just up the street and around the corner. Thank you. Thank you. Thank you! We ran back to the car, jumped in, and off we went.

We found the house easily, drove by it slowly and then around the block, checking it out a couple of times, trying to see how many people might have the same idea we did. There were a couple of parked cars, but otherwise it looked quite peaceful; so we talked it over and made the executive decision to go to a gas station bathroom to brush our hair and put on white lipstick so that when we saw them we *White Lipstick* would look good. It was around 9 p.m. when we got back, all glammed up for our adventure; it was a warm, summer night with a full moon. We parked and tried to figure out the best approach. It never, for one minute, occurred to us to knock on the front door. We knew from *Tiger Beat* magazine that wasn't how it was done.

Through a series of neighborhood adventures (which included meeting a 10-year-old girl who proved very helpful later on), we found the guest cottage belonging to the main house where the Beatles were staying ~ a small pink stucco cottage with white-trimmed windows and a brick patio surrounded by ferns and small orange trees. We had to get by the front door of that cottage in order to get to the path that led to the backyard of the Beatles' house. We weren't the trespassing type, so we knocked on the screen door to ask for permission to follow a path through their yard that led up to the main house and the Beatles.

The lady who came to the door was older, elegant, with white, upswept hair; she spoke slowly and had an accent like Greta Garbo in *Ninotchka*. She talked with us for a while and told us she was from Russia, was the daughter of a Russian princess, and had been a ballerina.

She said we seemed like nice girls, and it was fine with her if we went through her garden (the main house was hers, too, she'd rented it to the Beatles). SO happy! With leaping hearts, we turned to go, but then she said, "Just a moment, gulls (she meant girls), I should ask my husband."

The gulls slumped dramatically and took deep breaths, thinking *Oh, please don't do that.*

She called to her husband from the door, and "Reggie" came lumbering out, an imposing, craggy-faced man with fly-away eyebrows, and a permanently furrowed forehead whom I recognized as the English movie star Reginald Owen (appropriately, as it turned out, he once played Scrooge in the movie of the same name).

He looked at us, in our cute plaid skirts and bobbed hair, as though we had just dropped in from outer space. He frowned with an expression that said, *You brought me out here for THIS?*

The ballerina did all the talking.

"The gulls want to go up the back stairs and see what the Beatles are doing. We can let them do that, can't we, dear?"

He turned from her to look us up and down, shaking his head at what he saw and mumbling gruffly, "I don't think it's a good idea."

Crestfallen and a bit anxious (and already plotting an alternative plan ~ we weren't that nice), we watched him disappear back into the dim recesses of the cottage of doom.

The Russian ballerina, still beautiful and erect in her 70s (or something like that; she was probably only 40, but to us she was ancient and he was 165), saw how disappointed we were and put her finger to her lips as if to say "Shhhh" while stealing a furtive glance back through the screen door. She leaned toward us confidentially and said quietly, "Oh, gulls, he didn't mean that ~ you go ahead."

Karen

Wasn't that wonderful? I wanted to be just like her when I grew up. Blessings on you Mrs. Reginald Owen.

Up the stairs we flew ~ ducking down and running like soldiers across enemy lines, staying in the shadows while traversing the acre of garden that stood between us and the house. We got behind some bushes just in time to see the Beatles get out of the pool, dripping wet and lit by the full moon, wearing little tiny English bathing suits. They ran single file across the lawn, up the porch stairs, and into the house. We were paralyzed in our hiding place, clutching each other's arms, ears ringing, breathless at the sight.

Neither of us moved a muscle until after they were inside. Suddenly, Karen took off, she and her shadow zigzagging across the lawn, knees bent, staying low as she ran from bush to bush. Almost dying of silent laughter, hissing at her to "Stop it, please stop it," I followed her lead.

264

We got braver as we got closer to the house and realized we could see no one and no one could see us. We broke for the stairs to the porch that probably they called a veranda. It was a mansion, two stories, but the part we could see looked like this:

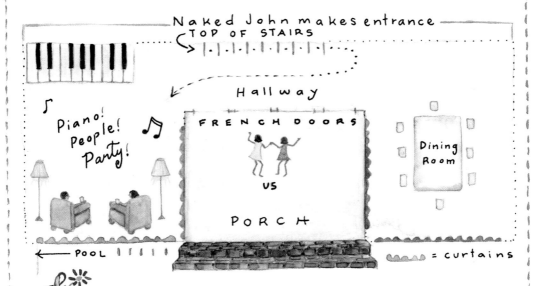

She curtains were closed in (what we found out later was) the dining room and also in the living room where someone was playing the piano and a few people were singing and harmonizing to the Everly Brothers: "Whenever I want you all I have to do is dream, dream, dream . . ." We could only hear, but not see, what was going on. Maybe it was the Everly Brothers!

There was a long bank of uncurtained floor-to-ceiling windows in front of us, with four French doors in the middle. On the other side of the glass we had a clear view of the hallway connecting the living room and dining room. Straight across from where we were standing was a staircase to the second floor. No one was in the hall or on the stairs.

We were sort of hanging out there, listening to the music, glancing through the windows while dancing, whispering, making up ideas of what was going to happen next, smothering our laughter almost to the point of pants-wetting, when suddenly there was movement inside. We stopped and looked up.

Bopping down the stairs, happy as a naked lark on birdbath day, came John Lennon, barefooted, no shirt, no pants, wearing just his underwear.

This was 1964, almost the very first day of the Swinging '60s ～ only yesterday it was the '50s ～ the swinging had not even really commenced yet, and we, at the time, did not see strange boys in their underwear. It was quite a shock, because after all he was a grown man and he was John Lennon. Plus, the worst thing was, we were having eye contact, and he was in his knickers (actually, to be exact, because inquiring minds will want to know, they were tightie-whities. I hope I pop no balloons with this inside information. You would probably rather not know. I know, that's how I felt).

I was so surprised. I stared into his eyes, shocked and speech-less, and he was pretty surprised, too, because, though he didn't stop moving, he looked right back at us. I'm sure he was thrilled to see us on his porch. Who wouldn't be?

At the bottom of the stairs, John turned and walked past us into the living room where the music was (do people walk around practically in their birthday suits at these parties? We had to wonder) and must have told someone about us, because

266

a man came and opened the door to the porch where we were still lurking (probably too weak to move) and sweetly said, "Girls, it's late, you should come back tomorrow."

And although we had come a mile and a day crossing the blurry line between reality and fantasy to get there, we said, "Oh yes, we're so sorry, we will." And off we went.

But we were happy. Because we saw the Beatles, almost naked, practically swimming, and, after all, we were invited back. Flushed with success, we drove home on the 405, down the hill into the Valley, a million tiny city lights in front of us, windows down, the big moon in a sapphire sky, KRLA on the radio, us singing along to Do You Want to Know a Secret including all the doo wa doos, happy happy happy, and plotting how we were going to do it again the next day.

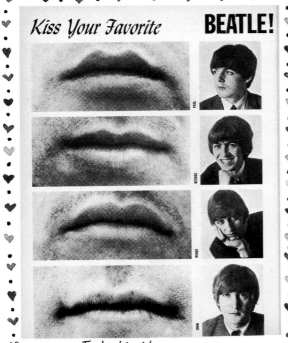

Kiss Your Favorite **BEATLE!**

Tucked inside my program

I spent the whole next day begging my father for use of the car. My mother was not qualified to give this kind of permission; it was above her pay scale. So I was forced to call my dad at his office. I was walking on eggshells, because my father didn't like to be called at work by his children, especially when we were in begging mode. But, as you can see, this was a teenage emergency, and I was willing to risk anything to get what I needed in order to be happy in life. And all happiness, at least for that day, depended on this one thing.

All day, it was No. No. No. No. And, no.

But Karen was depending on me. When I wasn't on the phone with my dad, I was on the phone with her, getting encouragement (ie, "But we just have to! Call him back!"). We never gave up and, FINALLY, around 4pm, the begging paid off. He said, OK, Yes ~ I could take the car (with about 50 rules attached). I leaped for joy and called Karen and screamed, "He said, YES!" We jumped in the station wagon and back we went, over the hill to Bel Air, on a mission.

By that time the whole world knew where the Beatles were staying. No parking was allowed inside the gates at all, Sunset Boulevard was a traffic jam, kids overflowed the sidewalks and swarmed the streets. We had to think, *How do we do this?* We found a parking spot a couple of blocks over and walked back through the gates. There were police on every street, but they weren't stopping anyone from walking around.

The other kids didn't know where to go, but we had experience and a general lay of the land. We went around the bend toward the house on St. Pierre and, as luck would have it, we ran smack into the 10-year-old girl I mentioned earlier, the one we'd met while exploring the neighborhood the night before, a neighborhood which this little girl knew like the back of her sweet little hand.

"Show us how to get to the Beatles' house from here?" we asked our new best friend, voices low in case anyone was listening (we wanted them to ourselves). "Only if you take me with you," she replied, quick as a bunny, LA girl, already genius at the art of the deal. The three of us turned into a side street, careful to ditch any onlookers or followers, and then, when we were in a good position and able to dodge the eyes of the police, we jumped into the bushes.

Up through the backyards we went ~ the kid leading the way. She bypassed the guesthouse completely and brought us in through another yard ~ we suddenly recognized our surroundings ~ then the three of us ran up to the porch where Karen and I had been the night before.

It was late afternoon, and this time the curtains were all open, as were the French doors. We could see in every room. There were maybe 15 people, all much older than us, some on the porch, some milling around the dining-room table; it was a little reception or something. But here we were, ta-daaaa, on their porch, like the Fuller Brush Man. I really don't know what people must have thought of us. It seems so rude to me now, but they were nice to us, said, "Hello, girls" ~ we almost felt expected; we definitely felt welcome. (Lucky for us, the concept of "stalker" was something from the future ~ there weren't even groupies in 1964.)

One by one the "boys" came out on the porch to say hello until we were more or less surrounded by them.

So good, to be surrounded by Beatles.

They were wearing tight black pants and buttoned-up shirts; George had on a vest. They looked like themselves, totally recognizable, all around 23, adorable, like their photos, with cute bouncy long hair and sideburns. They didn't know us, but we knew everything there was to know about them. We knew how old they were, that they used to be the Silver Beetles, that John was married and had a baby named Julian, and Paul had a girlfriend named Jane; that they went to nightclubs with "birds," they'd lived in Germany, and "gear" meant "good." We'd heard them talk on TV. Their Liverpool accents were even better in person.

Ringo spread his fingers on both hands and showed us his rings; and Paul, with his shiny hair, big eyes, and eyebrows like bird wings, shook hands with all three of us. (Of course, this means it's been over 50 years since I washed my hand, but hey.)

George had beautiful brown eyes and seemed shy, which made us even shyer.

John didn't seem to remember us from the night before, thank God. We did not want to relive the underwear incident. He was handsome with his clothes on; there was mischief in his brown eyes. He started showing off to the little girl, put his hands under his armpits, making his elbows into wings, which he flapped and then he barked, and we all laughed.

So great —laughing with the Beatles.

270

*O*ur nervousness and excitement about meeting them and finally being there, left us speechless (and I know for a fact I would be NO better at it if this all happened today). They tried to put us at ease, asking us how old we were and where we went to school; we managed to tell them we were just 17 ~ saying as few awkward words as possible, trying not to cry, faint, drool, or scream.

They offered each of us an autographed group picture (which, they told us, they signed on the plane over from England). I asked for an extra for my oldest sister, Paula, who was seven at the time and crazy about the Beatles, and they gave it to me. And then, like good girls, we left. Thank you so much, good-bye. Met the Beatles, check. ✓ We thanked

THE BEATLES

the little girl; she gave us each a hug and scampered off across the lawn, heading for home with a pretty good story to tell.

*W*alking back to the car through the manicured, tree-lined streets of Bel Air, we were jumping and leaping and twirling and making little screaming noises, when it suddenly occurred to us that what we had done could be illegal. If the police found out they *might* take away our autographed photos! So we quieted down and hid them in our clothes.

We walked by a policeman as unobtrusively as we could, but I guess he could tell we were excited or he heard our squeals from a block over, because he came toward us, eyes wide and twinkling, eyebrows up, very interested, like he knew, "Did you meet them?" He said it exactly the same way a 15-year-old girl would, almost shaking with excitement.

Despite the extra-large LAPD uniform, with gold badge and big black holster, in his heart, he was one of us.

And we said, "YES!" And pulled out our signed photos to show him; he was as thrilled as we were. "Wow, you got their autographs!" The big smile and obvious excitement of this grown man in a cop uniform made it even better. "Good for you, girls!" he said.

"Hey, they met them!" he yelled to his partner at the other end of the street, pointing with both hands at the tops of our heads. "All *right*," the partner hollered. Back to jumping and leaping and twirling and making little screaming noises we went.

We never saw the little girl again. We decided the only explanation was that she was our guardian angel.

We drove back to real life, over the hill, and into the Valley, with the windows down, wind blowing our hair, KFWB blaring *All My Loving*, the song the Beatles sang on Ed Sullivan ~ we knew it by heart. We felt so lucky, we felt changed, we felt lucky for life.

With luck on your side you can do without brains.
Giordano Bruno

$\mathcal{A}$nd here is still another real-life fairy tale:

$\mathcal{I}$n 1966, a couple of years after I met the Beatles, Janet and I rented an apartment in a small Encino complex next door to a man named Stewart who owned a company that trained wild animals for TV and movies: leopards, elephants, lions, tigers, and chimps. He was a gorgeous, tall Englishman whose girlfriend was Yvette Mimieux, the beautiful blond movie star, five years older than us, who starred in the movie *Where the Boys Are*. She would come over to visit Stewart and swim in the pool just outside our apartment door.

$\mathcal{O}$ne day Janet and I were inside our apartment, just hanging around, when Yvette walked across the patio in her pink bikini to our kitchen window and used it as a mirror. She had her reflection to keep her busy and was oblivious to us on the other side of the glass, but we were there, bug-eyed, giving each other the look of *Do you believe this? Yvette Mimieux!* She was the embodiment of sexy, classic movie-star beauty that we tried desperately (or would have tried if we thought there was any hope) to emulate.

As she fiddled with her hair and the ties on her bathing suit, I shrank back into the sofa, slid off to the floor, and crawled over to Janet who had fallen behind the breakfast bar; and together, on hands and knees we crawled around the side of the counter to peek at her without being seen. We were very mature (this is the period of time when we were trying to be ice skaters because of the little skirt).

Go away, little girl

273

While living at that apartment, I met an adorable co-worker and friend of Stewart's who turned out to be the wild animal trainer for the TV version of Tarzan, which was just beginning to film in Mexico. His name was Fernando, and he was from Mexico City. I was 19 and he was 26 when we fell madly in love and he bought me an airplane ticket to come down and stay with him at his parents' house while he worked on the show. I was excited about his invitation and said yes right away. But it was a foreign country. I'd never even been on a jet airplane, and I wasn't about to leave the country without talking to my parents, so I asked them what they thought about the idea.

Fernando at work

My dad called Fernando's dad to make sure everything was okay. Apparently he liked what he heard because he said it was fine. So I went! Got on the plane all by myself, asked the nun sitting next to me to hold my hands during take-off, and flew to Mexico City and to a whole new world.

I shared a room with Fernando's sister Tere (and her cat, Pipa, who loved me and wanted to sleep with me ～ an unrequited love, I'm afraid ～ I didn't know how heaven cats were then), in his parents' Mediterranean-style house with iron balconies covered in hot pink bougainvillea, behind high gates, where they had servants and a chauffeur and ended their phone calls by saying Ciao. (We never once said ciao on Claire Avenue, except maybe like in, "where's

274

the chow?") Fernando and his family and friends spoke three or four languages, Italian, French, English, and Portugese, in addition to Spanish. I spoke English and Arf and Arfy.

Fernando lived in the guesthouse in the garden with his older brother, Pepe. Among the upper classes in Mexico at the time, grown children remained living at home until they were married. If they didn't, the reputation and character of the whole family would be in question. I can't imagine what Fernando's parents thought of me and my family, out and about as

Fernando and me and the baby lions we got to take home for a night. You haven't lived until you've driven through traffic with baby lions loose in the car!

I was. I was way over my head in this cultured and foreign environment, but luckily, I didn't know it. It was all just wonderful and new.

I tasted ceviche and agua de limon and carne con crema, went to Churubusco Studios with Fernando every day to watch the filming, played with baby lions, and got to know Manny Padilla ("Jai"), Vickie ("Cheeta"), and Ron Ely ("Tarz").

Me with Manny Padilla who played "Jai."

275

Out to see the Mariachis

Fernando took me to nightclubs where we danced to Brazilian music, which I fell in love with. I loved all his romantic foreign "musica" ~ besides Brazilian (delicious Bossa Nova), he had lots of French and Italian records, music I'd never heard and, without him, probably never would have. He played his guitar and sang to me in Spanish; he introduced me to my favorite song for life, "La Vie en Rose."

I believe I learned my songs from the birds of the Brazilian forest. ♥ Antonio Carlos Jobim

We went to an elegant restaurant on a Lake called Del Lago, where candles reflected in the floor-to-ceiling windows, and every snowy white tablecloth was topped with a bouquet of yellow roses. There was a floorshow, about 30 violinists wearing tuxedos came out from somewhere, spread themselves throughout the restaurant and began playing "Some Enchanted Evening." I had Pheasant Veronique served from a silver-domed platter and Crêpe Suzette, which the waiter doused in Grand Marnier and Cognac and set on fire in front of us. Afterward, we went to a nightclub and danced to "Diablo con Vestido Azul"

276

and "Desafinado." How could a person not fall in love with all of this? It was magic.

Until Mexico, I'd never been out to dinner to

a nice restaurant in my life, so pheasant in grape sauce and flames at the table were quite an impressive experience for me. At the time, I did not know they lit food on fire. There were two forks next to the plates and two glasses to drink from.

Me and the babies

Fernando's family used cloth napkins in silver napkin rings, even at lunch, which they all ate together in the dining room. This was light years away from the chrome paper napkin dispenser on our table on Claire Avenue. I watched which fork they used; saw how they gracefully draped their napkins across their laps almost the moment they sat down, but I never mastered the one-handed-two-serving-spoon maneuver they used to serve themselves from a platter. I was from the Stewart Family Robinson School of Etiquette: stab it with a fork and shake it onto your plate.

As a 19-year-old swept into this foreign world, I spent most of the time in wide-eyed wonder. I wasn't happening to it; it was happening to me, like putting on the softest of cashmere sweaters for the very first time.

Best friends

277

Ron Ely was a doll in more ways than one, a perfect gentleman.

Tarzan went on location to Taxco, Tequesquitengo, and Cuernavaca, and I got to go, too. Fernando took me to a restaurant in Cuernavaca where I was given a cordial glass of Kahlua and cream that bubbled like a tiny volcano and tasted like heaven. During the day, I would go to the set, and while Fernando worked, I'd stay out of the way and watch the Lord of the Jungle thunder off on the back of an elephant, followed closely by Cheeta (and, in turn, out of the view of the camera, Fernando) to recover a serum stolen by a native chief ~ the only hope for Jai, bitten (in the episode only) by Fernando's lion and near death. It was thrilling but I took my book and hid in the back of a van while the lion was loose.

he crew went to Acapulco, and so did we. Acapulco was just a small town in 1966; there were only three hotels on the beach. We went out on a boat belonging to one of Fernando's friends where they made ceviche on board from just-caught fish, and to a palm-frond shack next

Tarzan is carrying Jai & Cheeta; Fernando's keeping his eye on Cheeta

to the ocean (just like the Big Kahuna's in Gidget) where I was the only girl among a group of guys singing and playing steel drums, guitars, and bongos while the sun set flaming orange into Acapulco Bay. Hello.

From Fernando's letter, September 19, 1966

A little action shot with Ron

"Tomorrow is going to be the worst day of my life as an animal trainer. We are doing a scene with two lions, a tiger, a jaguar, a leopard, a baby elephant, a big elephant, and two chimps. All in the same shot with Tarzan and they're all running away from a big forest fire, and me and Miguel and Morris, we're running after them to catch them. We'll be lucky if we get Vickie (Cheeta) back after the scene, so good luck tomorrow, Fernie Baby."

Pobrecito, I thought to myself.

279

Fernando wrote me wonderful, funny love letters that he signed "Te adoro" and I te adored him right back. In one of them, he proposed by asking me, "WHEN are you going to ask your parents how many horses and buffalo skins they want in exchange for their daughter, Susana?" I almost married him, came very close, but our lives were so different. He was 26 and I was only seven years past 12, and as I hope is clear, an idiot, and not ready for prime time. He was lucky to escape. Soon after I went home for the second time, he met someone else and married her instead.

I got the best of it, a wonderful experience, exciting new musica, a view of the larger world; plus, I tasted cilantro for the first time, ate delicious Mexican butter and sour cream, learned a few words of Spanish, got to pet a Bengal tiger, walk holding hands with chimpanzees, and play with baby lions. I felt love for another country and the warm people, was serenaded by Mariachis (*Cuando caliente el sol aqui en la playa . . . muy romantica!*), and ended up with a mere wisp of a broken heart, relatively speaking.

Me & Janet ~ my animal trainer days were short lived

I don't know why these things happened; they just did. I didn't really even think about it. It seemed normal the way they just showed up. We aren't in control of the circumstances of our childhoods. It would have been nice if my parents had spoken French instead of Arf and Arfy. I might have liked college and a reading list, sophisticated travel, finishing school, and a cultured environment, the things you read about in books; but we all get what we get, count our blessings, then do the best we can. My parents did that. They did the best they could with what life brought them, and I'm so grateful for every moment of my happy, care-free, innocent childhood. Looking back, of all the gifts I've been given, this one is my most treasured. I wouldn't change a thing.

All life is an experiment. The more experiments you make the better. ♥ *Ralph Waldo Emerson*

281

Falling in love with Cliff, marrying him, having our life together and those years ~ the time, the support and encouragement from him to learn to paint, to practice cooking, to plant my first garden, to be a homemaker, the freedom to do what I considered to be the most creative job in the world ~ was certainly more of that same kind of fairy tale, despite how it turned out. It was 10 years of following my heart, and still another huge gift.

But there I was, strapped in my lucky seat, streaking through the black sky toward the unknown. It was way past midnight, the glass slipper was lost, the carriage had turned into a pumpkin. I didn't know if I'd ever believe in fairy tales again. That life had come to an end (at least for the next three months), and the shock and pain of it were taking me to a whole other world. This didn't feel lucky, but it definitely was. Because the best was yet to come.

The fairies, as was their custom, clapped their hands with delight over their cleverness.
J. M. Barrie

I had just awakened from an exhausted sleep; my mind had been mingling dreams with memory. The stewardess was making an announcement. She wanted everything in an upright position; we were getting ready to land in Boston. I peered out the window into the pre-dawn darkness and saw the blinking lights on the wing of the plane, but no lights from below. I put on headphones, turned up the volume, held tight to the armrests, said a little prayer, and waited to see what would happen next.

*Up from the sea, the wild north wind is blowing
Under the sky's grey arch:
Smiling I watch the shaken elm bough, knowing
It is the wind of March.*

William Wordsworth

To be continued...

Go here
? ? ?
to see what happens
N E X T

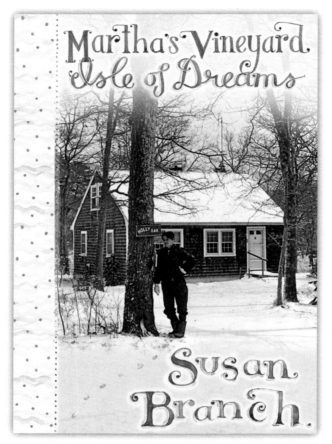

Martha's Vineyard
Isle of Dreams

Susan
Branch

PUB. DATE: Mother's Day 2016

A special thank you to my amazing, loyal, trustworthy and true blue "employees" (but really friends) at Susan Branch Studios, without whom I could never do what I do ~ Sheri Honeycutt, Alfredo Jimenez, and Kellee Rasor. I love you guys!

Thank you !

See how cute they are?

Musica

Thank you for a lifetime of inspiration. ♥

"Are you the reason my happy heart sings? But definitely..." ♥ Harry Revel & Mack Gordon

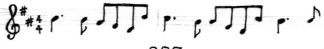

Adventures in Self Expression

singing, dancing, rhyming, story telling, drawing

Notes -
Started patty-caking at about 9 mo.
Played Peek-a-boo pretty good at about 1 yr.

Mother's Notes

First sentence
"Where's the baby?"
"See the baby."

Age - 16 months

Age - 16 mo.

First question
"Where's the baby?"

Repeats verses
"   stories
"   prayer   She said, "Now I lay me down to sleep etc.";
at 26 mo. all alone. We were quite
proud.

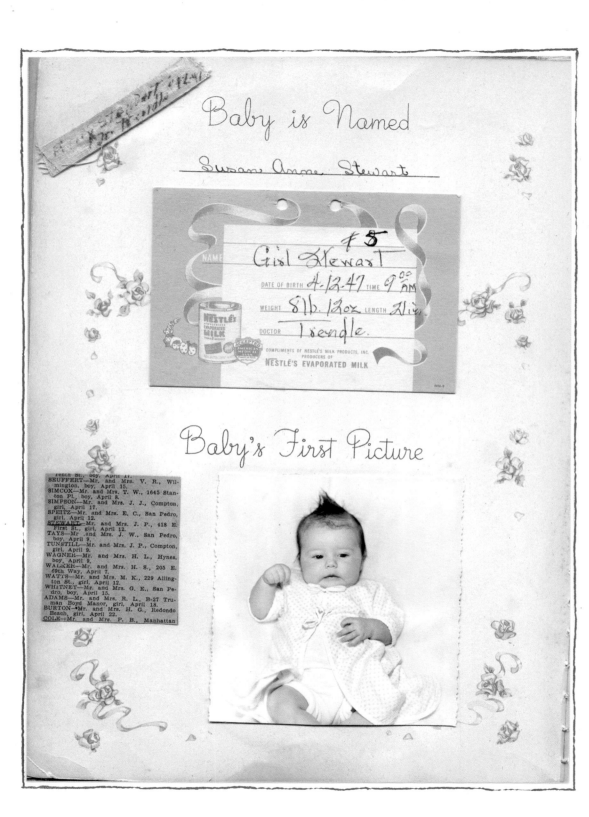

Baby is Named

Susan Anne Stewart

#5

NAME   Girl Stewart

DATE OF BIRTH 4-12-47 TIME 9:00 AM

WEIGHT 8 lb. 12 oz LENGTH 21 in

DOCTOR Trendle.

COMPLIMENTS OF NESTLÉ'S MILK PRODUCTS, INC.
PRODUCERS OF
NESTLÉ'S EVAPORATED MILK

Baby's First Picture